D0173333

PRIDE

YOU CAN'T HEAL IF YOU'RE HIDING FROM YOURSELF

DR. RONALD HOLT
DR. WILLIAM HUGGETT

Foreword by
VINCENT POMPEI, ED.D.

AUTHENTIC SELF PRESS

X

CONTENTS

PRIDE

YOU CAN'T HEAL IF YOU'RE HIDING FROM YOURSELF

By

Dr. Ronald Holt

and

Dr. William Huggett

Foreword By
Vincent Pompei, Ed.D.

Copyright © Ronald Holt, 2017

Foreword copyright © Vincent Pompei, 2017

All rights reserved.

No part of this book may be reproduced in any form or by any electronic or mechanical means, including information storage and retrieval systems, without written permission from the author, except for the use of brief quotations in a book review.

DISCLAIMER:

Neither the author nor the publisher assumes any responsibility for errors, omissions, or contrary interpretations of the subject matter herein. Any perceived slight of any individual or organization is purely unintentional.

The contents of this book are provided for informational purposes only, and should not be used to replace the specialized training and professional judgment of a licensed health care or mental health care professional. The authors cannot be held responsible for the use of the information provided. This book does not constitute the formation of a physician patient relationship. Please always consult a physician or a trained mental health professional for personal issues.

Self-help information and information from this book is useful, but it is not meant to be a substitute for professional advice.

Cover Design: Jennifer Stimson and William Huggett

Editing: Grace Kerina

PRIDE: You Can't Heal If You're Hiding From Yourself / Ronald Holt. -- 1st ed.

❦ Created with Vellum

ADVANCE PRAISE

"When I first met Ron Holt a number of years ago, he shared with me his goal of writing a book to support LGBTQ youth. What struck me was his passion, energy, enthusiasm, and knowledge of the subject – he's the perfect person to author this. This book exceeded my highest expectations. *PRIDE* is a powerful, practical, and important guide that will be a gift to everyone who reads it."

    –Marci Shimoff, #1 *New York Times* bestselling author of *Happy for No Reason*

"When I first met Ron, what impressed me the most about him was his passion, commitment, dedication, and genuineness in wanting to make a difference in and for the LGBTQ community. Ron used exactly those qualities when writing *PRIDE: You Can't Heal If You're Hiding from Yourself.* There is no question this book is going to make a difference in the lives of those who read it."

    –John Assaraf, *New York Times* bestselling author of *Having It All*

"When I was a talk show host on KABC Radio, Los Angeles, I often got calls from young LGBTQ people who were facing internal struggles and societal stigmas. Although I am a straight man, I am honored that they called me, and their pain shot through to my heart. Nevertheless, I never quite felt that I had the perfect resource to refer them to. I do now. Dr. Ron Holt, proud gay man and board-certified psychiatrist, *is* that resource. I recommend him and his book without reservation, to LGBTQ people themselves, and to those who love them. Dr. Ron is a gift."

—Joel Roberts, President of Joel D. Roberts and Associates, former prime time talk show host on KABC Radio, Los Angeles

"Dr. Ron Holt has shared his personal experience as a member of the LGBTQ community, as well as curated a collection of relatable stories that will inspire and encourage LGBTQ youth to know that they are not alone and have organizations, people, friends, and family members (genetic or chosen) to turn to. These stories, and the valuable lessons contained within them, will benefit a large section of the population that may not yet understand their worth, beauty, and health. I recommend this book for these people and the adults in their lives."

—Saul Levin, MD, former President of the Gay and Lesbian Medical Association and former Interim Director of Health in Washington, D.C.

"I first met Dr. Ron Holt in 2000 when he began presenting to Nebraska college students on LGBTQ issues. The information he presented was transformative for many students and life-saving, no doubt, for some. The heartfelt stories in *PRIDE* are inspirational for all people and are especially rich with hope, encouragement, and support for LGBTQ youth to live more authentic lives.

I highly recommend this book to anyone who would like to learn more about this important topic of our day."

Dr. Sheila Stearns, former college president and Commissioner of Higher Education

"Ron and I went to high school together. I knew Ron when he was struggling with continued harassment and bullying by his father. As a teacher, administrator, and now superintendent of a large school district, I have witnessed students and families work through many of the complex issues that Ron dealt with himself and that he addresses in his book. His book is a resource for all LGBTQ youth and their allies."

–Dr. James Sutfin, Omaha, Nebraska

"As he did in numerous, compelling lectures over the years, Ron Holt, Kansas City University adjunct clinical associate professor and alumnus, now brings the same compassion and insights to the pages of PRIDE. Through deeply revealing accounts of his own life, as well as the personal experiences of college students who share their stories, Holt provides practical advice for young readers – LGBTQ and straight alike – who struggle on the journey to self-truth, self-understanding and self-acceptance. Ultimately a universal call for unconditional inclusion among all in society, PRIDE beckons us to heed a true moral imperative of our day."

–Marc B. Hahn, DO, President and CEO of Kansas City University of Medicine and Biosciences

"I've had the privilege to collaborate with Dr. Holt in the area of healthcare equity for the LGBTQ community. I was particularly moved and inspired by his presentation on how to end suicide in the LGBTQ population. It has been a pleasure to watch him grow and expand his audiences over the years. Dr. Holt's book, *PRIDE*, is filled with precious life lessons, illuminated through vivid storytelling – truly captivating! This book is informative, relatable, and speaks to all people. It is especially useful for those who might be struggling to find their true identity. I highly recommend reading this book."

–Gayle Tang, MSN, RN, independent consultant and faculty, City College of San Francisco

"After seven years of running one of the world's largest anti-homophobia / pro-LGBTQ+ organizations, I finally have another invaluable resource to accompany my help and info pages on STOP-Homophobia.com. Dr. Ron is an inspiration to so many of us."

–Kevin P O'Neil, STOP-Homophobia.com

"I thoroughly enjoyed reading this book. As a leader in higher education, I highly recommend this book to my colleagues. This book is a powerful tool that can help positively impact the campus environment for faculty, staff, and students. The stories are compelling and provide a wonderful foundation to build upon. I compliment Dr. Holt on writing this much-needed book."

–Dr. Marysz Rames, President, Wayne State College, Wayne, Nebraska

"This book is the quintessential gift you will want to share with the young LGBTQ person who comes out to you. Dr. Holt is a healer; while working to heal himself, he has become a conduit of healing for young people across the nation and, most assuredly, in the heartland. His message of courage, hope, and unconditional love is one that inspires us all to live our truth."

–Karen Granberg, College GSA/PRIDE advisor

"Growing up in the Midwest, attending a rural college, and joining the Army during *Don't Ask, Don't Tell,* made my life as a gay man difficult and at times confusing. When I met Dr. Holt during my sophomore year of college, life got easier and clearer. His knowledge and insight strengthened my sense of belonging and helped me realize my importance. He fueled my confidence and empowered me to be me! For those who have not yet met Dr. Holt, his book provides strength and guidance."

–Sergeant Brent Ramsey, US Army

"I first met Dr. Ron Holt at an anti-bullying conference and was impressed by his wisdom in combatting bullying, particularly of LGBTQ youth. Because of this book, people who will never get to hear Dr. Holt speak will be able to benefit from his insights shared through relatable stories. *PRIDE* is a fast – and sometimes sad – read, but an important one."

–Walter G. Meyer, anti-bullying expert and author of *Rounding Third*

"I met Ron during our clinical training years. I could never have imagined that he would grow into the man whose heart and brilliance has given 'all of us' these important messages in his book, *PRIDE*. Ron's narrative, which is expanded into story, offers the reader a way to know the complexities that are faced by the LGBTQ community. Thank you, Ron, for your thoughtful, compassionate, and truthful writing. Ron's coming out story... it's painful, yet profound, and his honesty serves as the heart of this book."

–Dr. Nancy Hebble, psychologist

DEDICATION

This book is dedicated to the millions of LGBTQ youth and allies across the world who struggle for unconditional love and acceptance.

"Where there is love there is life".

—Mahatma Gandhi

FOREWORD

Today is unlike any other period in history regarding the LGBTQ civil rights movement and the advancement of awareness and knowledge about sexual orientation and gender identities.

When I was growing up as a teen, I found myself facing significant challenges accepting who I was. I felt suicidal and isolated, but there appeared to be no resources available and I certainly didn't feel comfortable coming out as gay – not even to myself. In college, my depression got even worse, so I made an appointment with a psychologist in the student health center. Coincidently, he happened to also be gay, and told me so. I remember feeling an enormous sense of hope. He was successful, kind, and, most importantly, appeared happy in life. Although he never knew it, he was my first gay role model and likely played a pivotal role in my survival, and in my success later in life. After just a few sessions, he encouraged me to join a LGBTQ support group on campus, which gave me additional tools and resources to better understand and embrace who I was.

Shortly after graduation, I became a middle school teacher and high school counselor. I quickly realized that anti-LGBTQ bullying and harassment were still rampant and that my colleagues appeared too uncomfortable or too unqualified to address it. I knew that I had to do something, but wasn't exactly sure how to start. I wasn't even sure if it was safe to be open about my sexual orientation at work, even though I was open to my family and friends by that time. Unfortunately, my fears came true when I got harassed by a fellow teacher, and then by my school administrator, due to them learning about my sexual orientation. Shortly after I reported the incident to the district office, I convinced the superintendent that mandated cultural competency training on LGBTQ students and staff was necessary. Within a few months, I was helping to train all district and school site administrators, and then staff at each school site. The visible change in school climate district-wide fueled my passion to do more.

I began to volunteer, after work and on the weekends, at organizations that focused on family support for LGBTQ youth and on suicide prevention. I then volunteered with the Center for Excellence in School Counseling and Leadership (CESCaL) to help put on the first national conference for school counselors focused on supporting LGBTQ youth. I eventually became the organization's first paid staffer and became the conference director. It was an amazing experience to watch the conference grow into a nationally renowned conference specially focused on improving the lives of LGBTQ youth. After four years with CESCaL, I was asked to help launch a national Youth Well-Being Project and annual conference for the Human Rights Campaign, the nation's largest civil rights organization dedicated to LGBTQ equality. The conference, titled Time to THRIVE, promotes safety, inclusion, and well-being for LGBTQ youth, and attracts educators, counselors, and other youth-serving professionals from across the country.

I first met Dr. Ron Holt in 2012, through a mutual friend. Ron offered to present a session on bullying and suicide risks among LGBTQ youth at the February 2012 CESCaL conference. His talk was well-attended and received, so I naturally said yes to him presenting at the conference the following year when he offered a session on the biological theories of male homosexuality.

A funny story is that, in April 2012, I was invited to, and attended, the White House screening of the movie, *Bully*, which was an amazing experience. While I was waiting for entrance into the auditorium for the screening, Ron and I ran into each other in disbelief, as we had both been invited to attend that special event. After sitting together at the screening, we had the privilege of meeting the Secretary of Education, Arne Duncan. It was such a fortunate experience for each of us!

Later that year, we were invited back to Washington, DC, to participate in the Federal Partners in Bullying Prevention Summit, where we were able to meet dignitaries from across the United States, and even Cynthia Germanotta (the mother of Lady Gaga), who spoke about supporting LGBTQ youth and ending bullying in schools.

When Ron asked me to write the foreword for this book, I immediately said yes. Ron is a board-certified psychiatrist, an openly gay man, and has years of experience speaking to and educating hundreds of college audiences. I can't think of a person more qualified than Ron to write this book on issues LGBTQ youth face.

In an easy-to-understand storytelling format, Ron presents facts and information on topics important to LGBTQ youth and allies, such as understanding that sexuality and gender are not things we choose; if and when it makes sense to come out about our feelings; emotional and physical issues that may occur if we don't accept ourselves; the importance of speaking our truth to our medical providers to obtain the best possible care; the effects of bullying on our health; and finding self-love and acceptance.

This book will benefit anyone who is LGBT or questioning their sexual orientation or gender identity. In addition, allies, friends and family of LGBTQ youth will also benefit from this information, to help support their friends and family. If you are struggling with your identity or want to support someone who is, this book is for you!

After reading this book, I encourage those who want to further support LGBTQ youth to attend the Human Rights Campaign's annual Time to THRIVE conference. This three-day conference is a one-stop-shopping opportunity to learn current and emerging best practices, as it brings together resources from over 45 national and grassroots organizations dedicated to supporting LGBTQ youth.

We certainly need more advocates to stand up and speak out for change so that all LGBTQ youth have an equitable opportunity to thrive!

Dr. Vincent Pompei
    Educator and LGBTQ Advocate

INTRODUCTION

I AM AN openly proud, gay man; married to the man I love; and I feel very fortunate to be living in a progressive city like San Francisco, a place where we feel comfortable to be open about who we are. We're enjoying career, financial, and relationship success. But, let me assure you, it was not always this way.

My earliest memories of being different from other boys go all the way back to the sixth grade. I remember that time as if it were yesterday. I was coming in from recess with the rest of my classmates, who were having a wonderful time discussing who they had crushes on and planned to marry one day. All of the boys were discussing their attraction to the girls in our class, and I simply could not relate to them. *Is something wrong with me?* I would often ask myself. I didn't have the same feelings toward girls my male classmates seemed to have.

It was then that I knew I was different from the other boys, but I didn't know why or how to put a label on it. Throughout my teenage years, I began to realize I was gay, but struggled tremendously with that newly understood reality. At the time, there were no openly gay role models that I was aware of. Those who were rumored to be gay were looked down upon and made fun of for being different and for going "against God's will." Because I was growing up in a conservative state like Nebraska, my fear of being discovered as "different" was an even scarier thought.

I grew up in a verbally abusive household where my father would not mince words about what he thought or felt about anything or anybody, including his negative views on homosexuality. I will share more about my experience of coming out to my father later in this book, but for now, let's just say it was much safer to be closeted than to be open about who I was.

Being closeted and unable to be myself, at times, caused depression, anxiety, isolation and even occasional thoughts of suicide. I adopted a very powerful fear-based belief that the world was inherently bad and could not be trusted. I came to believe the only way to survive was to hide who I truly was – even from myself.

In college, as I gained some distance from my father, I began to feel a slight bit of room to begin to acknowledge my deepest feelings. But I still felt that it was essential for my survival to hide my sexuality from others. Based on my experiences, I had mistakenly come to equate being gay with being weak. I had no intention of coming out to anyone, especially not to my father... but things don't always go as we plan.

Coming out to my father was one of the most terrifying, yet also the most freeing, events of my life. It was a freedom I had never experienced before.

Finally, when I was able to be true to myself and to my father, it felt like being born again. A powerful sense of inner peace came over me. In fact, I was reborn on that day and could finally start to live as my true authentic self.

Life is so very interesting. Sometimes our sweetest relief comes with the most bitter life lesson. My dad's rejecting response when I came out to him seemed to fortify those deep beliefs. Specifically, I believed that his reaction was what society at large felt about gay people.

Fast-forward many years to when my father died suddenly and unexpectedly. Unfortunately, we had not been able to work through our differences. So, in the end, I am left with a sense of remorse that he was not able to love me for who I am, but instead saw me as an enemy. I never want any youth to go through what I went through.

This is the first time I have put my experiences with my father in writing. I have always been afraid to share my story in such a public way, but at the same time I feel that this is much too important to remain silent about. Even now, after all these years, there are still young people who choose suicide over life because they are not accepted for who they truly are.

I have a doctorate in healing, but I am here to tell you the most important thing I've learned about healing. It may surprise you to know it has nothing to do with my knowledge of biochemistry or pharmaceuticals or my knowledge of Freud, Jung, or anyone else. The most important thing I've learned is that we cannot heal if we are hiding.

After coming out as a gay man, I decided to take the lessons and experiences I had learned from my adversity and turn them into an asset to help others. Although Lesbian, gay, bisexual, transgender and queer/questioning (LGBTQ) rights and awareness have come a long way since the time I came out, there are still tens of millions of people worldwide who struggle with their sexual orientation or gender identity. Many LGBTQ people struggle with various parental, religious, and societal pressures. Over the past several years, I have presented talks on LGBTQ issues. I admit I was initially terrified to speak out on a subject that I was so overwhelmingly frightened of back when I was a student. Over the years of presenting, however, I have come to embrace the adversity I experienced as a young, gay, closeted male, and have turned those experiences into an asset by helping others understand that they are not alone. Regardless of our sexuality or gender identity (GI), we are just as natural and "normal" as anyone else, and deserve unconditional love and acceptance. I have experienced tremendous growth and empowerment over the years by sharing what was once hidden in plain sight – my true, authentic self.

I am writing this book for those youth and young adults who are struggling to make sense of their feelings around gender or sexuality.

Through my presentations across the country, I have had the privilege of interacting with thousands of college-age students as we discussed and explored what it's like to be outside the heterosexual norm in society. I wish someone had come to my school when I was growing up, to tell me it was okay to be who I was, regardless of how I identified or saw myself. I am, therefore, writing this book to share my story and experiences in order to help others realize they are not alone and are worthy of love just as they are.

As a way of saying thank you for purchasing this book, I would like to offer you a free download of my LGBTQ coloring book, which is a companion book to PRIDE. For a free download, sign up at DrRonHolt.info. You can reach me about speaking engagements and book signings at DrRonHolt.com.

WHAT YOU'LL FIND IN THIS BOOK

I'VE HAD THE privilege of hearing, reading, and experiencing hundreds of real-life stories over the many years of my college presentations. I'll share my knowledge through storytelling, as a way of presenting material that you are, most likely, curious about. The information about me is real and based on my recollection. Each chapter's story that I've created is based on a combination of hundreds of compiled real-life peoples' stories that I have seen, heard, or experienced through giving my presentations. All names and locations in each story are fictitious. Any resemblance to any one particular person is purely coincidental.

This book is divided into six chapters.

Chapter 1 is the sharing of my struggles with growing up gay in conservative Nebraska. It is my hope that by sharing my story those of you who are currently struggling with similar issues can find comfort in the knowledge that you are not alone and that things will get better.

In Chapter 2, I approach the subject on the biology of sexuality and various aspects of the coming-out process.

In Chapter 3, I discuss the stress of being an LGBTQ teen. I also identify risks and review ways to develop coping tools against suicide. Included in this chapter is a discussion of how to deal with mental health issues that may arise.

In Chapter 4, I touch on how to stay healthy; how to take care of yourself; and how to know what to talk to medical/mental healthcare providers about in order to create a healthy life. I stress the importance of being open to providers so that they can give you the best care possible.

In Chapter 5, I share a story that deals with bullying and being victimized; discuss how to develop coping skills; and discuss resources that support LGBTQ youth.

In Chapter 6, I discuss finding self-love and finding acceptance, including how to embrace yourself and realize that you are not alone and are perfect "just as you are."

At the end of the book there's a reference section listing specific studies mentioned in the main chapters.

Although this book is tailored toward LGBTQ youth and young adults, in truth, it pertains to anyone who is hiding from who they really are; anyone whose "secret" prevents them from their truth. If you think about it, we are all hiding from something. Not living a true, authentic life for any reason can lead to similar outcomes and circumstances that LGBTQ people face.

Over my years of presenting, I have been asked numerous questions from audiences and on social media. I've incorporated answers to some of those questions through the storytelling in this book, as they pertain to the different chapters' contents. I am almost certain that information asked of me in the past is the same type of information you are curious about, too.

I have received countless written comments from students and others about how my presentations affected their lives. It's immensely rewarding to receive comments from people who's lives have been positively impacted from material I have presented. Much of the same information is in this book. And I hope you it equally helpful in your journey.

1

MY COMING OUT

I'VE ALWAYS BEEN hesitant to share my coming-out story, and hadn't imagined writing about it, but I never want any other person to go through what I went through. Even now, after all these years, there are still people who choose suicide because they aren't being accepted for who they are. I simply cannot remain silent any longer.

Growing up, I had a very difficult time dealing with the constant berating of gay people by my father. It definitely made my coming out to my parents a very difficult decision. Hearing continuous homophobic comments made it near impossible to accept myself for who I was. Hiding and denying my sexuality felt like the only option.

I can certainly tell you that hiding my sexuality, which is such an essential part of who I am, took a great emotional toll on me.

I grew to have a tremendous fear that my other family members held the same beliefs as my father. Reaching out to my brother, mom, or extended family was not an option, because it didn't feel safe to do so. Had I admitted my sexuality to my father while I still lived in his household, I strongly believed he would have told me to leave. I would have been out on the streets, which – at the time and at such a young age – was a terrifying idea.

With the education and hindsight I now have, I believe my parents knew I was gay when I was very young. However, to acknowledge, let alone accept, me as his gay son would have been far too frightening for my dad. Rather than allow me to embrace my sexuality while growing up, my father made my home a threatening environment in which to come out. I felt I had to stay in the closet if I wanted to stay at home.

I realize that coming out to family and society can be a very scary idea for a lot of people. Although we may come to understand our sexuality at a young age, it is not always easy to find the support or encouragement to come out – especially when we are struggling with self-acceptance and self-love. Being true to ourselves does lead to better health and internal happiness, but there is a time and a place for coming out – and that time may or may not be now for you.

The purpose of this chapter is not to tell you whether or not you should come out, but to help you decide what is right *for you* about how, when, or if to come out. Even if you don't feel like you have a lot of control over your life right now, you are the only person who can ultimately decide how it is lived.

So let me tell you more about my story.

My Story

I knew from a very young age that I was not like the other boys who talked about how excited they were about girls. My earliest memories of being different go all the way back to the sixth grade. I knew I was different then, but I didn't know how to put a label on it. As the years progressed, I slowly began to realize I was gay. It was a terrifying notion in part, because there were no known openly gay role models in the community at the time. The only thing I knew about gay people was how they were portrayed in the media, and the derogatory comments my father would make.

In my teenage years, my feelings only intensified. I struggled tremendously in solitude and never officially came out as a gay person to anyone. But my secrecy didn't stop my father from tormenting me. He would frequently bully me and call me names like "fag" as I was growing up.

After years of that abuse, I was depressed, anxious, and isolated. Whenever I told my dad that I had thoughts of killing myself because of how he was treating me, he would say, "Go ahead. You don't have the balls to do it." I adopted the belief that the world was inherently bad, no one could be trusted, and the only way to survive was to hide who I truly was – even from myself.

During all of my youth and young adulthood, I grew up hearing negative comments from my father about being gay, which I incorporated into my sense of self-worth. Before I knew it, I had internalized homophobia – a hatred of myself and a tremendous fear of being associated with gay people. I thought, *If it's not safe to be my authentic self in front of my father, then it surely won't be safe to be open in public.*

Throughout junior high and high school, I desperately attempted to fit in with the crowd, but deep down inside, my soul was dying. I so desperately wanted to fit in, but didn't know how and certainly didn't feel safe to try to do so. I continued to be bullied and ridiculed by my father throughout junior high. This led to further withdrawal and isolation. I never really fit in with the other male students and often found myself feeling more comfortable gravitating toward friendships with girls.

In high school, I attempted to fly under the radar. The fear of being "discovered" as gay was always present and often took most of my emotional energy throughout the day. On the outside, I looked like I had everything going for me: passing grades, athlete, involved in extracurricular activities, as well as being involved in church. By no means was I considered a popular student, and this actually made it easier for me to keep my secret. On occasion, I would be called "gay" or "fag," in playful or not so playful ways. Even though I would attempt to play it off or seem indifferent to the comments, deep down inside it felt like a knife was stabbing me. The fear of being outed or discovered was terrifying. Being teased and bullied only confirmed, in my mind, the learned belief that being gay was bad and immoral.

As many youths do who are being bullied, I identified with the aggressor and would often lodge homophobic insults towards others in an attempt to get the attention off of me. *After all*, I thought to myself, *I'm not really gay if I tease others for being gay*. That's a common thing that some gay people do when they are struggling with their own acceptance, and it is an example of how internalized homophobia can occur.

There were not any gay-straight alliance (GSA) or queer-straight alliance (QSA) support groups on campus at that time and, to my knowledge, there were no openly gay role models in my high school. There were rumored to be gay teachers, but being gay was nothing to be proud of, let alone openly accepted.

When I was growing up, I never imagined having the opportunity to muster the courage to accept who I was, much less let others know I was gay. Based on the open hostility I experienced from my father, I knew it wasn't safe to be open about who I was until I was, at least, graduated from college and on my own financially – even if that meant living on student loans while continuing on to medical school. The idea of coming out to my father while still even somewhat financially dependent on him during college was simply not a safe option.

I started dating my current husband in secrecy toward the end of my sophomore year of college. He had just graduated from the college I was attending and had moved away to Omaha to attend medical school. Over the next three years, we saw each other whenever we could on weekends, school breaks, and during summers. We also spoke on the phone every day that we could. Having a long-distance relationship is hard enough – let alone having a long-distance relationship in secrecy. Although my parents knew Bill and I were friends and had met him, neither Bill nor I were out to our families. We, therefore, had to sneak around when we were together, so as not to raise suspicion from my parents.

During summer breaks, I attempted to spend as much time as I could with Bill, but my family living in the same city as Bill made it difficult. It was always very uncomfortable not being able to tell my family that I was hanging out with Bill.

When I graduated from college, I applied to medical schools that were close to Omaha but not in Omaha, so that I could continue to see Bill, but be far enough away to give me some distance from my father. Looking back at that time now, I was planting the seeds of independence from my father. It was time for me to feel more free to start living the life I deserved. The medical school I chose was in Missouri.

Medical school was a new challenge, from an intellectual point of view. It was even more challenging for me because of my worries that someone in my class might discover my deep secret of being gay. Due to the way I was brought up, I had mistakenly come to equate being gay with being weak. I had no intentions of coming out to anyone else at that time, especially not to my father in the way it ended up happening.

On a cold December day when I had just finished the final exams for my first semester of medical school, I called my father to arrange my trip back to Nebraska for the holidays. I planned to spend time with my family over the holidays, as I had done my entire life. During our conversation, my father lapsed into one of his all-too-familiar gay-bashing tirades, talking about someone else in a hateful way. He had done that many times before but, for some reason, on that day, something woke up inside me. Rather than listen passively, as I had done so many times before, I spoke up. I told him that I didn't agree with the way he was stereotyping others. That simple comment led to more conversation and, before I knew it, he asked me point blank if I was gay and if Bill was my partner.

I had rehearsed that moment endless times over the years in the event he every outright asked, but, in spite of all my planning, I was completely thrown off guard. Never in a million years had I thought of coming out to my father over the phone.

But that inner voice, deep down inside me, rose up and, with all the courage I could muster, I blurted out, "Yes!"

Then I immediately thought, *What did I just do?*

"Fine!" my dad responded. "You have chosen this life, and you are never welcome home again!" And he abruptly hung up the phone.

A powerful wave of deep calm and inner peace came over me. It was like nothing I had ever experienced before. Finally, I had been able to be true to myself and to my father. I thought to myself, *If losing my family allows me to be open and honest about who I am, then it's worth the price.* Even though I wasn't going home for Christmas that year, I was rejoicing deep in my soul. I was reborn that day and could finally start to live as my true, authentic self.

Transformative as that experience was, it was also the start of one of the most challenging periods of my life. Soon after I came out to my father, he started making harassing phone calls, each time leaving intense and, at times, threatening voicemails. They ranged, from the man I called "father", insisting that I listen to my mother as she was wailing in the background, to him informing me that he was contacting an attorney to have my last name changed, because he felt I had brought shame and embarrassment to the family.

Although I still felt empowered by having come out to him, his words fortified the deep belief I still carried that his opinion was what all of society felt about gay people.

His next phone call was a message that the rest of the family was going to be tested for HIV, as being gay somehow equated to having the virus. As the days progressed, the voicemails escalated, and became even more frightening. My father threatened to out me to my entire medical school administration, in the hope that I would be expelled from school.

And then my father descended to a place I would not have thought possible between a father and his son: he threatened to kill me. And my partner. That message sent chills down my spine. Since Bill was living in the same city as my father at that time, I immediately called to warn him. He was at the medical school, but skipped classes, packed a bag, and drove to Missouri to be with me. Unfortunately, we let our fear get the best of us. We fled my apartment because we were afraid my father might drive to Missouri to kill us.

We were hiding in a nearby hotel, with little money and no plan for what to do next. Bill and I frantically searched for help to deal with this craziness. We finally found a gay-affirmative pastor who sat down and spoke with us. After our conversation, he said he would reach out to my father on our behalf. He did speak with him, but my father was bent on destroying our lives. The next day the pastor told us he had never spoken to someone so full of rage.

The harassing phone messages continued to come in multiple times a day. Finally, after a few more days, we felt as though we couldn't run any longer, so we returned to my apartment, where we still felt alone and afraid. The low point occurred one evening as Bill and I were sitting on the sofa in my apartment. We felt so alone and afraid that we actually talked about committing joint suicide. But it was in that place of fear and despair, that a tiny flame of light and strength was ignited within us. We decided that night not to end our lives.

The next time my father called, I harnessed this newfound strength and interrupted his tirade. I told him if he threatened us again, I would go to court, report his behavior, and obtain a restraining order against him. Finally, I stood up to him and his bullying. As is often the case with bullies when their violence is exposed and others stand up to them, he crumbled into a heap of his own fear and shame. My father never harassed us again after that day.

Several years later, while my father and I were still out of touch, he died suddenly. I was left with a sense of sadness that he had never been able to love me for who I am. He persisted in needing to see me as an enemy.

Even though I was out to my family by that time, I was still closeted to most of the rest of my world. Shortly after finishing my residency training in San Francisco, I began working as a clinical psychiatrist. Working initially for a large medical corporation gave me a sense of anonymity that allowed me to keep my sexual orientation private. But, as the years progressed, I began to understand that there was more work for me to do in the realms of self-acceptance and self-love. All the training I'd received to help other people heal wasn't going to do me any good unless I was able to heal myself.

Society often seems to expect that a psychiatrist is going to have it all together. But I learned that I had to go through my own personal healing, and healing would need to be done in a way that no structured training could teach. I had to transcend the very field I was trained in. And I had to stop hiding.

As I stopped hiding and began working through those horrendous experiences with my father, I was able to begin to embrace who I was at a deeper level. In the following years of extensive personal work, I went through a transformation toward self-acceptance and self-love. Although that work is far from complete, I have profoundly improved my sense of self-worth and come to believe that the most challenging adversities in life can be transformed into the most powerful assets. I can say with confidence that this type of transformation can be an amazingly empowering journey.

Let me share some tips with you on how to transform the adversities in your life into assets.

You Cannot Heal If You Are Hiding

After coming out to my father, I felt like a new man. Although his reaction was one I would never wish upon anyone, I wouldn't change that opportunity to come out from hiding. Looking back, I can see that hiding who I was had been making me feel worse and more prone to emotional pain and stress.

As humans, we often have truths that we are afraid to come out with, and we've all worried about disappointing others. That can be true no matter what we're hiding. You might be hiding feelings around your sexual orientation or gender identity, your love for someone else, abuse you may have endured, the need to end a relationship because you can't be your authentic self within it, or a myriad of other human dilemmas. Despite these fears, you must speak up, at least to yourself or to another person in a safe context. The point is, you cannot heal and become your true, authentic self until you stop hiding.

The good news is that the courage to be authentic is something we all have, even when it feels, at best, only like a faint flicker of light buried deep within. That courage is there because, at our core, we know that true healing – and our true lives – can't begin until we are free to be open about who we truly are.

Forgiveness Is a Gateway to Peace of Mind

Although I will never forget, I have come to forgive my father for how he treated me. Maybe he had never been given unconditional love himself. I realize now that, for whatever reason, my father simply didn't have the capacity to be the person I needed or wanted him to be. For many years, I held onto a deep resentment and even a hatred toward him. But I've slowly come to the realization that my resentment and hatred weren't hurting him; they were only hurting me. I found that I couldn't move forward with my own life until I forgave him. So, I feel grateful that, today, I can say that I have forgiven him.

We all know what it's like when we hold onto feelings of anger, resentment, or hurt. These feelings might eat away at us for days, years, or even an entire lifetime, if allowed, and we end up suffering if we can't release them. In order to heal, we must realize that even though we can't change the way someone has treated us, we *can* change the way we respond to their behavior. When we release resentment and anger, we are then able to take back the power we had surrendered. *One of life's great paradoxes is that we can regain our personal power when we forgive those who have hurt us.*

You don't have to forget what happened, but moving forward with forgiveness brings deep healing. Forgiving someone is not done for their benefit, but for your own. Letting go of negative feelings gives you the profound freedom to move forward and fill that once-negative space with feelings of love. It's a boundless type of love that transcends the individual self. Forgiveness opens up space for renewed relationships with yourself, with others, and perhaps even with the person who hurt you.

Sometimes, the tables are turned and we have hurt someone else. In these situations, forgiveness is an important part of the healing we can offer to those we have injured. When we ask the other person to forgive us, we are inviting them to experience the transformative healing that comes when they let go of the pain they are carrying.

Empowerment Comes from Sharing Our Truth

After coming out and eventually forgiving my father, I decided to turn the lessons I'd learned into an asset to help others. Although gay rights and awareness have come a long way from the time I came out, there are still millions of people who struggle with their sexual orientation or gender identity. So, for the past several years I have been traveling back to colleges in the Midwest to give presentations on lesbian, gay, bisexual, and transgender issues.

I have to admit; I was initially terrified to speak on the subject I'd been so frightened of back when I was a student. However, over the years of giving these presentations, I've come to embrace the adversities I had as a young, gay, closeted male. I've worked to turn those painful experiences into an asset by helping others understand that they are not alone, and their sexuality is just as natural as anyone else's. I have experienced tremendous growth, empowerment, deeper connections, and self-acceptance over the years by sharing what was once hidden in plain sight: my true, authentic self.

We each have unique knowledge, skills and abilities that can be used to help others, but sometimes it's the adversities in our lives that turn out to be our biggest assets. Sharing an adversity and letting others see what you've experienced can be frightening, but with time, it will be empowering for both you and the recipient of your message. You can share your message in countless ways. The important thing is to speak out about your adversity and be open to the ways it can help you and others learn and grow.

I've come so far from my days of living in fear and hiding who I am. I hope my story helps you stop guarding any secrets you might have—and start living a truly authentic and fulfilling life.

2

BORN THIS WAY

GROWING UP IN conservative Nebraska was very challenging for me. Not only was I struggling with my sexual feelings from a very young age, but I was raised by a homophobic father, all of which prevented me from discussing my feelings in a public way. Looking back at my life now, I wish I would have had access to information relevant to how I was feeling, including what it meant to be gay, and the questions I asked myself, like *Am I choosing these feelings? Why am I this way?*

I can remember having a lot of struggles as a young kid. My deepest feelings just did not feel "right." There were no labels for me to attach to what I was feeling back then, but I did have a distinct sense that I was different because of those feelings.

Added to that conflict and confusion was the fact that I was born to a man who seemed to be Nebraska's most homophobic father. To call him homophobic is even a huge understatement. This man could espouse hatred from every pore of his being.

I barely need to tell you this, but there was obviously no space in our household for me to ask questions or try to figure out the feelings that seemed so much a part of who I was. I would have done anything to be able to have the information that I'm going to share with you in this chapter.

Life's most despairing challenges often gift us with the most beautiful insights and opportunities for growth. That was certainly true for me when it came to my experience growing up as gay – both in Nebraska and in my family. Although a lot has changed in our society since then, young people still struggle to make sense of their sexual feelings deep inside of themselves.

Over the years, I've given lots of presentations to young people and I'm deeply touched by every story they've shared with me. Many young people share with me how they feel that their sexuality is not "okay," or that there is something wrong with them because of who they find themselves attracted to.

It's my deepest desire to try to help you have a better understanding about the feelings you are having. It's my hope that by the time you finish reading this chapter, you'll have a deeper appreciation for all that you are and will know that you are worthy of love.

I'd like to tell you about Jim.

Jim's Story

Jim was a 17 year old college freshman in rural Nebraska. He grew up in a small town in the middle of the state, where the rural farm economy has been on the decline for years. There were just over 1,000 people in his hometown.

For as long as he can remember, Jim wanted to fit in, but it was clear to everyone that he was not the smartest, most talented, or most popular boy in town. He had deep yearnings of wanting to escape, but he didn't really know what that would look like.

Sometime around the sixth grade, Jim began to notice that he was having feelings that seemed different from what the other boys were talking about. Jim didn't seem to be too interested in the budding sexual development of the girls in his class. But he did seem to be more and more interested in hanging out with a few of the other boys.

One boy in particular really caught Jim's attention. His name was Mark.

While Jim was quiet and in the background, Mark was outgoing and the life of the party. Jim had little to zero athletic prowess, while Mark excelled at any and all athletic endeavors. Jim had very few friends, in contrast to Mark, who was so popular that almost everyone was his friend.

Jim's family had been active in the evangelical Christian church in their town. Mark's family was active in the Catholic church, which was the only other church in town. There wasn't much open conflict between the two faith communities, but there was certainly an unspoken innuendo in each camp that viewed the other group with a bit of disdain. The one thing that seemed to unite the two groups was their common enemy – homosexuality.

Jim had grown up in his church hearing sermon after sermon about the evils of homosexuality and about the "perverts" that were most certainly going to hell. He often heard the phrase "Love the sinner but hate the sin." He never could quite understand that strange statement. For Jim, his deep feelings were so much a part of who he was that he couldn't understand how people could hate the "sin" and not also hate him. He so desperately wanted to talk with someone, anyone about his feelings, but it didn't seem like there was anyone he could turn to.

Jim had two older brothers who had no problem fitting into the small-town culture of going out on Friday nights after football games, getting drunk, and flirting with whichever cheerleader put up the least resistance.

Deep down, Jim felt repulsed by the ways his brothers behaved. Yet it seemed like everyone else looked up to them. That made Jim feel like even more of an outsider. There was absolutely no way Jim could ever confide to one of his brothers about his deeper feelings.

Jim didn't feel he could turn to his parents either. They were decent enough folks. They had both graduated from high school, which placed them in the upper echelon of education in their community. They were both pretty stressed about providing for their sons. By the time Jim was born, they seemed more exhausted than enthused about parenting.

It seemed like the only option for Jim was to keep his feelings hidden from everyone. As a result, he felt it was safer for him to steer clear of others altogether, lest they find out what he was hiding. He longed to be able to talk to Mark, but Mark seemed to always have it together. Jim felt here was no way Mark could relate to what Jim was feeling.

As Jim went through high school, he distanced himself more and more from other people, from his secret passion for music, and, ultimately, from himself. There were many nights he quietly cried himself to sleep. His only solace was in journaling. He would write down his deepest, most secretive and shameful feelings. And he wrote love letters to Mark. In the confines of his journal, Jim could be a full-time musician and Mark was his most devoted fan. He knew that Mark would never read the letters, but in the act of journaling a whole new world of possibility was open to Jim.

Jim wished he didn't have his feelings. But no matter how hard he tried to be free of them, they didn't go away. So he kept writing in his journal. Because of that, he developed a love for writing. In the world of his journal, he could finally be free. He could love and be loved. But he still felt confused because his writing didn't help him understand what his feelings actually meant. He didn't have a clear label for his feelings, and there were certainly no role models in his community.

Then, one day, Jim's world took an unexpected dive. His mother was folding and putting away Jim's laundry and she happened upon his journal. She knew looking at it was something she shouldn't be doing, but once she read the first few sentences, her heart dropped to her stomach. She couldn't stop reading, even though the pain inside of her grew with every word she read.

His mother felt she had to do something. The only thing she could think of was to talk to her husband and then with their church pastor. The three of them were waiting for Jim in the living room one afternoon when he came home from school. Instantly, he knew what was happening, but he didn't yet know the horror that was about to unfold.

After the three adults confronted Jim with the "sin" of who he was, he was more or less coerced into "spiritual counseling" through the church, in an effort to rid him of his "sinful" feelings. He really didn't feel he had a choice at that point. The world around him had become aligned with the deep self-hatred that had been growing inside of him for many years.

For the next year, Jim went to religious-based counseling and prayer sessions with the pastor. He was told that if he repressed his authentic feelings toward men, he could return to the arms of the religious community and, therefore, be free. Therein was the big lie, because if we turn away from our authentic feelings, we are never free. No matter how hard he tried, Jim couldn't manufacture sexual desire for women. With the coaxing of his pastor, Jim agreed to a truce. He would renounce his sexual feelings for other men and live out the rest of his life without sexual feelings.

For the first few months after "successfully" completing church counseling, Jim appeared to be excelling in school. He had deeply repressed his true feelings by then and was living the life his parents and pastor wanted for him.

As high school progressed, most of Jim's classmates began to date and have romantic relationships with each other. Jim attempted to date women, but, deep down, he felt like his soul was dying. He was attempting to develop feelings towards women, but it simply didn't feel natural to him. Jim found himself becoming increasingly depressed and anxious as high school progressed. He began to isolate himself, which caught the attention of his parents.

His parents wanted Jim to be happy, so they encouraged him to start dating a girl named Lisa, who he knew from church. He had known Lisa since grade school. She was sweet and seemed interested in Jim. He wanted so much to develop romantic feelings for her, but no matter how hard he tried, it just didn't feel right.

Jim found himself sliding into a horrible abyss. He wanted to make his parents happy, so he continued dating Lisa, but felt he was creating more and more of a lie. He was lying to his parents, to Lisa, and to himself. Finally, Jim saw no way out of his predicament and he started planning a way to end his life.

Those thoughts scared him enough that he mentioned them in passing to his mother one day as she was busily getting ready for work. Hearing Jim mention that he actually wanted to die was the ultimate cold splash of water that woke up Jim's mother. She realized they had not been helping their son. Instead they had been cornering him into a place from which Jim was willing to escape by ending his life.

At that point, Jim's mother made an appointment for him to meet with a licensed mental health counselor. Over the next few months of talking with the counselor, Jim was able to finally find hope.

The counselor helped Jim think about applying to college. He had always felt, deep down, that there had to be something more in life. He knew he needed to grow beyond the narrow walls of the only life he'd ever known. As he started to come to terms with his most authentic self, he started to feel more comfortable with his sexual feelings. That opened up the possibility that he could, in fact, go to college – and maybe even pursue a degree in music.

He would be the first person in his family to pull off going to college... if only he could hold it together long enough to graduate from high school. Fortunately for Jim, and with support from the counselor, he was able to do that. He was accepted to a college in a small town in north-east Nebraska. Mark had also been given a full-ride baseball scholarship to that same college. Although the two young men would be in two different worlds in the same college, Jim felt comforted by the knowledge that he would be able to be on the periphery of Mark's very full life.

The college town was a bit larger than their hometown, and only about an hour's drive from where they had grown up. But, to Jim, his childhood journaling seemed to be pleasantly unfolding in his college experience.

The college Jim enrolled in is one where I regularly present lectures. I speak to various groups there, such as the psychology and education departments, the athletic department, and faculty audiences. One year, I gave a presentation to Jim's psychology class. Jim sat in the very back of the lecture hall as I presented on the topic of the biology of sexuality.

Jim learned that all the way back in 1973, the American Psychiatric Association had declassified homosexuality as a mental disorder, because there was no scientific evidence demonstrating that it was an actual disorder. He learned that conversion therapy, also known as "pray away the gay," or "reparative therapy," has been debunked as a form of therapy.

Jim learned that what he had been put through was not uncommon. Treatments that attempt to change a person's sexual orientation have never been shown to be effective. Many people like Jim had been able to repress their feelings but, unfortunately, just like with Jim, they paid a price when those important, very real feelings were repressed. Jim came to understand that these types of therapies have been determined to not only be unproven, but harmful. Almost all schools of mental health now consider that type of therapy as a form of pseudoscience.

With this new information, Jim now had words to help him understand the confusion he had lived through. Even though he had been able to date Lisa – and even have sex with her – he had no real sexual desire for her or for women. Jim came to understand that repressing his feelings towards men did not change his sexual orientation. It only changed his sexual behavior, which did not feel natural to him.

That day, he learned about numerous studies that have explored the subject of sexual orientation, including studies about male siblings raised together. Recurring findings show that, for non-identical twins, if one male sibling is gay, there is a 25% chance the other male sibling will be gay. For identical male twins, if one twin is gay, there's a whooping 50% chance that both twins will be gay [1]. Jim was equally amazed by the findings of a literature review I did of six twin studies that were done in the 1990s and 2000, showing that the occurrence for homosexuality was greater in identical twins than in non-identical twins.

An interesting fact that Jim learned, and that he felt applied to him, related to research studies that demonstrated a correlation between birth order of male siblings and male sexual orientation. A well-known scientist referred to this phenomenon as the "older brother effect." The research showed that the more older brothers a man has from the same mother, the greater the chance of that man being gay [2]. Some estimates are that 15% of the male homosexual demographic is associated with this effect.

Finally, Jim learned that many studies have shown actual differences in brain anatomy between gay and straight men, as well as differences between the brains of straight women and lesbians [3][4]. There are also studies that show differences in the chromosomes of gay men [5].

Jim walked out of the presentation with the realization that there was a lot more he wanted to learn. He discovered that I was giving a presentation the next day on the subject of coming out. While the first lecture had been part of his psychology course, the following day's lecture was completely optional, and open to the general public.

At my lecture about coming out, I shared my personal story. During the question and answer session after my presentation, Jim learned even more about issues he had dealt with, along with some he had not yet sorted out. We explored the answers to questions such as: *Am I comfortable with who I am? Why come out now? Can I be patient with the reactions of my family and others? Is it safe to come out at school and/or home? Do I have a support system? Who should I tell first?*

As Jim absorbed my story, he contemplated ways he could come out safely, and when. He heard my praise of the campus PRIDE (People Respecting Individuals, Diversity, and Equality) group. This group offers heartfelt support for anyone who is beginning to navigate the coming-out process.

Before enrolling at that particular college, Jim had done some research and learned about the existence of the PRIDE group. During his research, Jim had learned that membership in the PRIDE group was confidential and by invitation only, after being interviewed by the group's faculty advisor. That level of screening made the group seem safe, and joining it seemed like a great way for him to receive the peer support he yearned for. Jim knew it was time to join as his next stage of self-acceptance, and to help him navigate his own coming-out journey. He decided he would reach out to the PRIDE group's faculty advisor.

Jim listened carefully during the discussion of how a parent can help set the groundwork for a child to come out. He agreed that coming out, at any age, can be a very difficult and complex decision. He could appreciate that most people likely struggle for many months, if not years, with decisions around if and how to come out.

Jim felt comforted to learn that we begin to identify with our sexual attraction towards others around puberty, when we are ten to thirteen years old. That helped Jim understand that his feelings, all those years ago, had been "normal." Even though one can begin to identify with their sexual or emotional feelings around the age of ten, that doesn't always mean that someone embraces those feelings, and they may not fully accept them until later in life, if ever. Jim was surprised to learn how some trans youth can identify being trans as early as three to five years old, although some may not identify as trans until much later in life. It made sense to Jim, because he could see that we are all different in our maturation, background, and self-acceptance. It gave him peace to realize that people can come out as gay, bisexual, or trans at any age.

Jim agreed when he heard it takes a tremendous amount of trust for a person to come out to a family member or friend. The most important words a parent will say to their brave child, are the words immediately following their child's disclosure of their sexual orientation. Those words will have an everlasting impact on both the life of the child and their relationship with their parent. Making judgmental or rejecting comments at that important moment of disclosure can have a devastating impact on the child's life, including raising the risks of mental health issues, substance abuse, and even thoughts of suicide. Words can never be taken back. Jim wished that his mom had access to the information he was learning. He imagined how much she could have helped him if she had only had known these things.

Unbeknownst to Jim until much later, his mother was sitting on the other side of the auditorium, feverishly taking notes throughout my presentation. She had read about my public presentation in the local newspaper. As the session ended, they both left quietly, through separate doors, neither of them aware of the other's presence on that day. And yet, now that they both had that new knowledge, they knew their lives would never be the same again.

After absorbing the information from both my lectures, for the first time in his life, Jim realized that his feelings were not something he had chosen. He started to see that the God he had been taught to believe in had, in fact, created Jim, including his unique brain structure, his chromosomes, and even the effect of having older brothers. Those were not things Jim had chosen. He found himself feeling more connected to the beautiful being that was *Jim*, and he finally started to feel a real connection to other people who had gone through their own journeys of coming out.

He recalled how helpful his licensed therapist back home had been. Although Jim had grown a lot in the past few months since starting college, he felt it was time to start connecting more with other people.

As he walked back to his dorm room, Jim smiled at the memory of watching several YouTube videos only a year ago. The videos were part of the It Gets Better campaign. When he'd first heard that message and seen those videos of people's stories about how it got better for them, he didn't believe it could apply to him. But now he felt completely different about it, because he could see a bright future for himself. He was living proof that it *does* get better.

With a warm glow inside, Jim sat down to write in his journal, which was in a password-protected app on his laptop. That day, he did not put his journal entry in the software app. Instead, it took the form of an email. What's more, it was a love letter. It was a heartfelt love letter to Mark. The words and feelings flowed out of Jim's heart. He was overcome with feelings of love and hope. Jim felt alive for the first time in his life. As a tear of joy rolled off his cheek, he smiled to himself and hit "send".

* * *

IN JIM'S STORY, you read how people do not choose their sexual orientation and there is no proven way to change sexual feelings. Attempting to hide or change what feels natural to you causes more harm than good. There are many factors that contribute to a person's sexual orientation, but conscious choice is simply not one of those factors. Knowing this will hopefully give you the confidence to embrace who you are.

There are many things to think about when considering coming out. Coming out is a personal decision that should occur only if and when you are ready.

Remember that, no matter your sexual orientation or gender identity, you are worthy of unconditional love and acceptance.

3

MENTAL HEALTH

IN THIS CHAPTER we'll look at some subjects that are important to know about, regardless of where you are on your journey. I'll share a story about some areas that have to do with mental health.

We all have different goals and aspirations in life, but we do have some things in common. We want to be happy. We want to have people in our lives who love and accept us for who we really are. And we want to feel that our lives matter.

Some people experience these positive feelings automatically, while others struggle in life to feel grounded in positive ways. Some people undoubtedly have good self-esteem, and feel loved and accepted. Most often, that is because they have loving parents, families, and friends who support them.

Unconditional love and acceptance are extremely important. Unconditional love is a powerful gift to give and to receive. Life can be difficult when a person doesn't feel loved. Feeling loved, feeling as if we fit in, and having supportive loved ones around us are para mount to helping us feel that our lives matter.

In Chapter 1, I told you about my experience of growing up. It was difficult for me to try to fit into a heterosexual society while living a hidden life. I felt isolated and deathly afraid that someone would find out that I was gay. I didn't have the internal resources to accept myself back then, and I considered ending my life.

My story is not at all unique. In fact, there are millions of LGBTQ young people around the world who are struggling with many of the same issues I struggled with and that you may be struggling with, too. Even though some in society have become more supportive, there are still too many instances of sexual minority youth who are bullied, harassed, and victimized. People are still dying, either by their own hands or by others, because of who they are.

It can be very stressful to navigate life as a member of a sexual minority group. This stress can lead to problems like depression, anxiety, substance use, low self-esteem, physical problems, and suicidal thoughts. All of these experiences are made worse when a person feels that they need to hide because they are afraid of being rejected or even harmed.

I want to tell you about a young person who thrived after coming out at a young age, and the consequences she endured from having to go back into hiding.

Bria's Story

Bria was born and raised in Brooklyn. She was the youngest of five kids. Her next oldest brother was six years older than she was, so Bria grew up more like an only child. Her mother worked as a paralegal in a large, prestigious law firm in New York City and her father had a successful sales career with a solar technology company.

Bria's mother had moved to the U.S. from Puerto Rico when she was eighteen. She had desperately wanted more for her life than the poverty in which she had grown up, just outside of San Juan. Bria had been told about her aunts, uncles, and cousins on her mother's side, but they all still lived in Puerto Rico. Her mother told stories about growing up in poverty and how important it was for Bria to do well in school. Bria's mother had achieved a great deal, but she knew her daughter had the ability to accomplish even more.

Bria's father did not have any living family. He had been born and raised in rural Georgia during the late 1960s and had gone to school in the 1970s, when racial segregation was still the norm. Bria never knew her grandparents on her father's side. They had both died by the time she was born. Even though she never knew her grandmother, her father's mother, there were many stories that had been passed on about this woman.

That grandmother was described as a strong woman who'd fought against racial inequalities during at a time in U.S. history when it could have gotten her killed. Bria's grandmother had been filled with conviction to do what was right, and she'd had the internal strength to carry it out. Her courage was much larger than her diminutive physical stature. She was said to have a thousand times more courage than all the cowardly KKK thugs that hid behind their masks and harassed her family while she was growing up.

When it was time for Bria's grandmother to go to high school, she was one of the first African American students to attend an all-white high school back in the 1950s. Although Bria never knew her grandmother, throughout her childhood, there remained a deep sense of respect for that woman that permeated Bria's family's home. Bria seemed to have a connection with her grandmother. When she was little and her older siblings were off doing their own things, Bria would talk to her grandmother and could almost feel her presence.

As she grew up, Bria continued to feel connected to the spirit of her grandmother. Although she didn't realize it, Bria was being groomed to play an important role in her generation's fight for civil rights. When she was twelve years old, Bria realized that she had feelings for both boys and girls. In many families, that would be a big problem, but, fortunately for Bria, her parents were very supportive. They made sure she knew without any doubts that they loved her unconditionally. They embraced her fully as the beautiful, strong, and courageous young woman she was growing into.

With that solid foundation of family love and support, Bria was able to come out as bisexual at her Brooklyn middle school. With the support and encouragement of her friends and several teachers, she helped to start the first GSA at the school. When she became a freshman and started high school, she had all kinds of support from her friends and teachers. She joined the high school's well-established GSA.

Bria was exceptionally talented in debate and was near the top of her class academically. She had great friends and enjoyed school and family life. She knew, deep down, that she was going to follow her older siblings who had all gone to college; two of them had gone on to graduate school. Bria imagined that, one day, she would go to law school. She wanted to become a corporate attorney. Her mother had worked as a paralegal and Bria's dream was to become a partner in that prestigious firm.

Bria's father was also successful in his career. He was slowly climbing the corporate ladder in the sales division of a solar energy company. That particular company had regional offices across the United States, and his dream had always been to become Vice President of sales in charge of his own regional sales office. One night, when all of Bria's brothers and sisters were home for dinner, her father announced that he'd finally received the promotion to Vice President of a regional sales office.

The family was ecstatic, as was Bria, until one other detail was revealed. The position was in South Dakota. They discussed options to have Bria stay in New York with one of her older siblings, which would enable her to finish school in New York. Bria loved her older brothers and sisters, but she knew they were all busy with their own lives and starting their own families. The alternative was for Bria to move with her parents and finish out her senior year in a new school.

Bria kept sensing what felt like her grandmother's spirit gently nudging her. That nudging was for Bria to move with her parents to South Dakota. So that's what she decided to do.

Bria was reluctant to let anyone know just how frightened she was about the thought of moving to the Midwest during her final year of high school. She anchored herself with the stories of her grandmother going into the all-white school in the 1950s. Bria realized that the move could be her opportunity to experience something similar to what her grandmother had gone through. She was determined to face the challenge with the same amount of courage that her grandmother had shown all those years ago.

So, during the summer year before Bria was to start her senior year in high school, she and her parents moved to South Dakota. Bria was anxious for school to start so she could make new friends. But her already shaky confidence was shaken even more when she noticed how few people of color lived in that community.

In fact, the only other person of color Bria met that summer was an older Latina named Dominga. Dominga worked as a custodian at the high school. Bria met her one day toward the end of summer when she was trying to find the location of one of her classes. Over time, Dominga became Bria's only real friend. It was as if Dominga knew all about Bria, even though they didn't really talk much. Their conversations consisted mostly of Dominga rambling on about her life. She described how she had fled the civil war in Guatemala in 1988 with her three boys, explaining how fearful she had been of her sons being conscripted to fight in the war. She came to the U.S. with no money and then worked hard as a custodian to support her family.

Dominga told Bria many times how important education was. She repeatedly told Bria the story of how she had wanted to go to school to become a social worker, so that she could help other immigrants. Her dream was to pass on all that she had learned from her hardships to future immigrants. Dominga had a deep desire to help make their lives better than hers had been. However, she had to work in order to support her three sons, which meant Dominga was unfortunately never going to be able to fulfill her educational dream. Although it was too late for her, she repeatedly reminded Bria that now it was Bria's opportunity for education.

Even though all three of Dominga's boys were now on their own and very successful, which afforded Dominga the opportunity to stop working, she told Bria that she continued to work at the school because she felt it was her mission in life to help young people like Bria. Dominga felt a calling to help whoever she could. She felt it was her job to pass her educational dream on to any student who was willing to take the torch from her and carry it further than she had been able to.

Over time, Bria got tired of listening to Dominga ramble on. She really wanted to meet someone her own age. She couldn't wait to join the debate team and, of course, the GSA.

Soon after school started, Bria searched for, but couldn't locate the place where the GSA met. She asked several people and, each time, had to explain that GSA stood for Gay- Straight Alliance. Bria started to wonder if the school even had a GSA. She finally realized they didn't have one, had never had one, and didn't have plans to start one.

Recalling the stories of her grandmother, Bria decided she had an opportunity to follow in her grandmother's footsteps. Bria went to her school counselor, Mr. Bradshaw, who did triple duty as a high school counselor, assistant football coach, and faculty representative for the Fellowship of Christian Athletes (FCA). Initially, Bria was reassured when she learned that Mr. Bradshaw was involved with the FCA. Back at her high school in New York, she had developed great relationships with several of the faculty members who sponsored the Christian groups. They had all been very supportive of her work with the GSA and, together, they'd taken on projects to help homeless youth in Brooklyn.

Full of confidence, Bria walked in and explained to Mr. Bradshaw that she wanted to start the first ever GSA at the school. Upon her announcement, Mr. Bradshaw got a slight crinkle in his brow and snapped his neck back, as if he'd been zapped with an electric current. His eyes shifted away from Bria. He looked down and mumbled something about how the school had never had a GSA.

Bria said she was well aware that the school didn't have a GSA and that was why she wanted to start one. Mr. Bradshaw went on to say that the reason the school didn't have a GSA was because "All the *normal* kids never really had a need for that kind of thing." He said it was highly unlikely that the school board president, who was also the minister of a large Baptist church, would "approve of a group that promoted alternate sexuality."

Now it was Bria's turn to be shocked. Her jaw dropped. Mr. Bradshaw noticed her reaction and shifted the conversation away from starting a GSA. He suggested it would be easier for Bria to fit in if she could be "a little less 'in your face' about this gay stuff."

Bria couldn't believe what she was hearing. For the first time in her life, she felt what she had always imagined her grandmother must have felt on her first day of school. *This is how it must have felt when my grandmother walked into the all-white school*, Bria realized. She imagined walking through a gauntlet of teachers and students who made it abundantly clear they wanted her to disappear or be someone she was not.

Because of that meeting, Bria understood that she was in a school that pretty much wished she wasn't there. So she came to the conclusion that it might be better if she hid her sexuality from everyone until she graduated from high school and could move away. However, the rumors were already flying.

Bria decided to try out for the debate team. As a junior back in Brooklyn, she had been the captain of the debate team, so she thought she'd have no problem making the team at her new school. During the tryouts, Bria knew in her heart that she was by far the most articulate and strongest debater.

On the afternoon that the debate team members were announced, Bria was utterly shocked when she didn't even make the team. She was crushed. She ran into the bathroom to hide because she was so close to tears. Bria was terrified to let anyone see her cry. Crying in public was something she wouldn't let herself do. As she sat in the bathroom, silently crying to herself, she heard two girls come in. They were elated that they had both made the debate team.

Bria overheard one of them say, "I'm so glad we're not going to have to put up with that gay Mexican chick who thinks she's all that."

Bria sat in the stall for what seemed like hours that afternoon. She was paralyzed. After a long while, she heard the bathroom door open and snapped back to reality. It was the unmistakable clamor of Dominga, rolling in her cleaning cart to clean the bathroom. Bria could not face Dominga, not today, not like this.

She waited until she thought she could sneak past Dominga and made a quick dash for the exit. Just as she thought she'd slipped past without Dominga noticing, she heard the older woman begin to speak. Dominga didn't even look at Bria; she just kept mopping the floor. Very softly and reassuringly, Dominga said to Bria, "Ser fuerte, mi niña," which means "Be strong, my child." Bria desperately wanted to be strong, but this was all too much for her. She ran home and went straight to her room without saying a word to her parents.

Over the next few months, Bria longed to be back in New York. The once academic all-star was now failing some of her classes. She found herself becoming more isolated; she couldn't sleep at night; and she dreaded every new day, for fear of what it would bring.

Her parents watched as their cheerful, bright young daughter spiraled into the abyss of depression. They were finally able to get Bria to open up and share with them what she'd been going through at school. Her parents took action right away and made an appointment to meet with the high school principal.

The principal said she would talk to the students who had been bullying Bria. Unfortunately, the teasing, bullying, and harassment only got worse after that. One day, a large note was taped to her locker that said, "Oh look. A closet. Get your ugly butt back in it!" Bria turned around to see who might be looking at her as she peeled the note off her locker. She felt ashamed, even though she was the victim. She asked herself, *Why does everyone hate me so much?*

Bria turned and walked with her head down to her first class of the day. She often tried to wait until after the bell rang to arrive at school, so she wouldn't have to be in the hallway with the others students before class started. That cut down on the time they'd have to insult her, at least in her presence. She longed for the comfort of the huge inner-city high school back in Brooklyn. Even though she had been one among thousands of students, she'd felt safe and accepted in Brooklyn. In this new school in South Dakota, all she could focus on was not if, but when the next attack would come.

Bria didn't know how she was going to get through the rest of the school year. It was too late for her to transfer back to New York; she'd fallen too far behind and if she transferred back, she would have to repeat most of her senior year.

Bria began sneaking into her parents' supply of alcohol. She only wanted to be able to sleep at night. She found the alcohol calming enough to allow her to fall asleep, at least for a few hours. She didn't know any other way to calm her nerves. It wasn't long before the drinking had increased to binge level on weekends.

As her parents saw Bria's downward spiral, they reached out again to the school's principal. This time, the principal recommended that Bria be seen by "a mental health doctor who could maybe get her on antidepressants to help her to get along better with the other students." Even though Bria's parents were appalled by that response, they thought it might help Bria to be able to talk with someone. They were desperate and wanted to help Bria however they could, so they made an appointment for her to see a psychiatrist.

The psychiatrist was a man named Dr. Ed Grove. He was old – way older than her parents – and Bria couldn't imagine ever opening up to him. But, over a few weeks, his grandfatherly style started to reassure Bria that, even though he probably couldn't help her, at least he was harmless.

Over time, Bria did slowly begin to open up. She started to refer to him as Dr. Ed, which he didn't seem to mind. Eventually she told Dr. Ed all of what she had been going through. They talked in detail about what it had been like for her. Then, one day, Dr. Ed said that he wanted to tell Bria something.

He started by telling Bria how he always tried to maintain a space for the client in psychotherapy sessions, and had a policy not to share his private information with his clients. That day, however, he said he wanted to share something with Bria. He told her that, several years ago, his youngest daughter had come out to him and told him that she was lesbian. His daughter told him about the pain she had suffered as a result of remaining silent and hiding her sexuality from him. He came to realize first-hand how damaging it could be for a person to feel that they had to hide who they were.

He also told Bria that his daughter had been killed a few weeks after she came out to him. She was killed in a hate crime because of her sexual orientation.

Dr. Ed told Bria that he was going to do whatever he could to help her get through the struggles she was experiencing. Because of his story, Bria believed him and began to open up more.

The two of them talked about Bria's depression and alcohol abuse. She began to understand that those painful experiences were directly related to the feelings she was trying to hide. Bria was trying to be someone she wasn't and it was threatening her physical and emotional health.

With that new awareness, Bria began to have hope and she quit drinking alcohol. But, unfortunately, she couldn't figure out how she could possibly be out in her school. She decided she would try to get through the rest of the school year and remain hidden. She would live as fully as she could while trying to convince herself and everyone else that her bisexuality was only a temporary stage for her. She even agreed to go to her senior prom with her male chemistry partner.

The prom started out okay, but later in the night when the alcohol and weed were passed around, Bria overheard her classmates making comments about her. She noticed several classmates whispering and pointing at her while they giggled to themselves. That escalated until the captain of the cheerleading squad walked over to Bria and called her every vile name Bria had ever heard.

Bria ran out of the prom. Her date helped her home and wanted to stay with her and help her, but she asked him to leave. She sat alone in her parents' house, still buzzing from the alcohol and marijuana. She looked at herself in the mirror and her memory flashed to Dominga telling her to be strong. Then she imagined her grandmother walking through the school hallway full of white people jeering at her. Try as she may, Bria simply couldn't be strong any more. It was all more than she could take.

Bria went into the living room, grabbed a bottle of vodka from the liquor cabinet and used it to gulp down a handful of over-the-counter sleeping pills. She was done. She just wanted to go to sleep and never have to face anyone ever again. It wasn't long before she passed out.

Several hours later Bria awoke in the emergency room. Her parents were talking to Dr. Ed, who had been called by the ER doctor. Dr. Ed was standing there talking to her parents, in what looked to Bria like his pajamas. Dr. Ed and her parents looked at Bria without saying a word. She could see and feel the love and concern in their eyes and on their faces. In that moment, as she felt the support they were so obviously offering her, Bria's memory flashed again to Dominga and to the images of her grandmother. However, this time Bria thought to herself, *I **am** strong. This is my challenge and, somehow, I **am** going to make it.*

Lying there in the hospital bed, Bria didn't quite know what she was going to do next. She had, for all intents and purposes, given up on going to college. Even though she had outstanding SAT scores from her junior year, she had pretty much lost all of her motivation over this past year in the new school. She hadn't even applied to any colleges. However, that all changed for her that night in the emergency room.

She now had what she called her Committee of Five. The Committee was made up her parents, Dr. Ed, her grandmother, and Dominga. With their help, she was determined to finish her high school education and go on to college. She was more committed to studying because she was more determined than ever to become a lawyer. Bria wanted to fight the injustice of discrimination. In her moment of utter despair, she had found a new source of strength.

Over the next few days, Bria scoured the Internet for nearby colleges. She went on a last-minute whirlwind tour of all the local colleges that were still accepting students for the fall semester. One of the colleges she visited was in northeast Nebraska. It was as if she had been guided to visit that particular school on that particular day, because, as she was touring the school, she noticed a flier in the student commons. It was an advertisement for a talk that I was presenting that very day on the topic of LGBTQ suicide. Bria decided she had to attend the lecture, even though it wasn't part of the official tour the school had organized for prospective students.

Although Bria wasn't yet enrolled as a student, she embodied what must have been the spirit of her grandmother as she strode into the lecture hall that day. She had the confidence and poise of a world leader. She sat down in the front row and took copious notes throughout the presentation.

Bria eagerly listened as I described the warning signs for suicide. She realized that she had been exhibiting a lot of those signs herself in the months before she even consciously felt at risk for suicide. She learned about the increased risks of substance misuse when a person is a member of the following three groups and facing significant discrimination in our society: females, minority races, and non-heteronormative sexual orientation [6]. Bria belonged to all three groups, and she could relate, as she reflected on how she'd used alcohol in an effort to numb her emotional pain.

She could also appreciate how bisexual youth can be at higher risks of suicidal thoughts, because of the rejection they can feel from both the heterosexual and homosexual communities. Bria could personally relate to information that LGBTQ youth who are victimized are at higher risks for suicidal thoughts and attempts [7].

I covered many other topics that day. One thing that really struck Bria was how important it was to have supportive family members and friends. Knowing that support was a strong protective factor in helping young LGBTQ people get through the challenges they face made it clearer to Bria just how important it was to have GSA-type groups in schools. It was not about making a political, religious, or even a social statement; rather, it was about keeping other young people like herself safe and alive.

What resonated with Bria as she listened to the presentation was how detrimental hiding can be to a person's mental health. She finally understood that her depression, substance abuse, suicidal thoughts – all of it – had begun shortly after she started to hide who she truly was.

Bria wasn't able to write down all of the things she had learned that day, but as she got up to leave the lecture, she realized she had been given a new mission for her life. She heard me talk about how I had taken my most intense struggles and turned them into an asset to help others.

Her path became crystal clear to Bria that day. She knew she was going to get her undergraduate degree, go to law school, and become a lawyer. But instead of becoming a corporate lawyer, she was going to specialize in civil rights. Her new life mission was to help expand basic human rights for the LGBTQ communities. She felt strong enough to take the torch from those who had gone before her. Bria was going to devote her life to fight for those who were not yet able to fight for themselves.

As she walked out of the lecture, she reflected on her Committee of Five, recalling and feeling the love and support her parents had given her and the kindness of Dr. Ed. She chuckled as she remembered his appearance that night in the emergency room. Then her memory shifted to Dominga and how Bria would now confidently carry the torch that Dominga had so gently passed on to her. Finally, Bria looked into the blue sky and felt her grandmother's spirit smiling down. She could sense her grandmother looking down on her and seeing the beautiful strong person that Bria had become.

Armed with a mission, as well as a new sense of self-worth, Bria couldn't wait to graduate high school and join the GSA at the college where she would soon become a student.

* * *

IN THIS CHAPTER, Bria's story showed us the importance of knowing both the risk for and the protective factors that guard against suicide. We learned that hiding what feels natural can cause emotional distress, including suicidal thoughts.

Most importantly, we learned how having support can have a huge positive effect on someone who's struggling. With loving and accepting support, the need to hide is greatly reduced, and strength is found.

4

PHYSICAL HEALTH

OVER THE YEARS, I've had the privilege of speaking with thousands of clinicians and medical students about LGBTQ health. It would be a mistake to say that the health care needs of the LGBTQ population are exactly the same as their straight peers. LGBTQ people are at higher risks for certain mental and physical health issues, which puts them at higher risk for health complications, if left untreated.

The LGBTQ population is not at higher risk only because of their sexual orientation or gender identity. Their higher mental health risks stem from the need to hide their identity from society. Their physical health risks come from inadequate health screenings and lack of access to competent care. Therefore, their mental and physical vulnerability leave them at risk in profound ways.

As we saw in earlier chapters, hiding what feels natural to us can lead to various stressors in our lives. Hiding your sexual orientation or gender identity from health care providers not only makes it more difficult to form a trustworthy bond with your provider, but also prevents your provider from screening you for issues that may be more important to your specific health needs. The discrimination, judgment, victimization, and harassment that LGBTQ people face also put them at higher risk for health issues. When there is not adequate support, people tend to cope through unhealthy lifestyle choices, such as drug and alcohol abuse, smoking, and other unhealthy coping mechanisms, as a way of self-medicating.

Throughout my adolescence, and even into early adulthood, I did not have a conversation with my pediatrician or primary care physician about my sexual orientation or gender identity, nor was it ever asked on any forms in the doctor's office. I think the possibility of coming out to my doctor, or at least talking about my feelings, would have been more feasible if the clinic environment had welcomed and invited me to do so.

In this chapter, I focus on keeping yourself healthy, and discuss the consequences to your health when not being true to yourself.

Pat's Story

Pat was born and raised to a working-class farming family in central Iowa. His father was a hard-working farmer who worked the land that had been in the family for generations. Pat had two older sisters and four older brothers. His older brothers worked on the farm with their father during every free moment they had outside of school. Although Pat appreciated his brother's desire to teach him the chores on the farm, Pat felt more comfortable staying inside, helping his mother around the house and playing with his sisters. Mom was a devoted housewife who took care of everyone in the house, making sure no one went without clean clothes and three meals a day. Mom was thrilled when Pat was born, as she loved the idea of raising another son.

Pat was considered an independent child who, nevertheless, loved to follow his mother around the house and actively participate in whatever she was doing.

Toilet training was a challenge for Pat. From a very young age, he insisted on using the bathroom in private and felt uncomfortable peeing in front of his brothers. Mom shrugged it off, thinking it was simply Pat being shy – a shyness she herself had struggled with while growing up.

As preparations were made to enroll Pat in preschool, he made it clear to his mom that he did not want to wear jeans, instead he preferred wearing his sister's old dresses and playing with their dolls. After numerous arguments about appropriate clothing for little boys, Pat relented and wore boy's clothes, as his mom requested. Although he would participate in the activities the other little boys did in grade school, he always enjoyed getting home, jumping into a one-piece sleeping gown and playing with dolls.

Pat began expressing interest in girls in junior high and dated female classmates in high school. Although he truly enjoyed the company of females, he felt very distant from his male anatomy and had no interest in sexual intercourse.

During high school, Pat's next oldest brother, Dave, publicly came out as gay. Dave was only a year older than Pat. And even though Pat was younger, he had developed a protective instinct towards Dave. They had always been super close growing up, so Pat showed unconditional love towards his brother and became an advocate for LGBTQ rights by starting a GSA group at their local high school.

In spite of some support from Pat and a few others, Dave struggled to come to term with his sexual orientation. He went through significant depression and anxiety during the time he was becoming aware of his same-sex feelings. Because there had been no openly gay role models in junior high, Dave had felt isolated and alone. On weekends he'd found himself dabbling in alcohol and smoking his dad's cigarettes, as a way of self-medicating. Because of the hangovers Dave experienced some weekends while binge drinking, he quit attending the gym and quit the junior high's track team. Dave's mom became worried when she noticed that Dave was gaining weight and withdrawing from people. She made an appointment for him to see the family pediatrician.

Dave hadn't come out yet to anyone except Pat. He really wanted to be honest with his pediatrician, but he was too afraid of being judged. He looked for clues in the doctor's office that would indicate the medical office was affirming toward LGBTQ people. Dave looked for things such as a rainbow flag or a pink triangle in the waiting or exam room. He saw nothing. Even the intake forms had no questions about sexual orientation or gender identity.

As his doctor entered the exam room, he said, "How's it going Dave? It seems like there have been some changes since I last saw you. Your mom seems concerned about you."

"Oh, you know, doc, just some stuff..." was the extent of what Dave felt comfortable revealing.

During the physical exam, the doctor noted a 25-pound weight gain, a new cough, and an enlarged liver. The pediatrician became more concerned and told Dave, "Your body is telling me that there's more than just 'some stuff' going on in your life. I want you to feel like you can talk to be about what that 'stuff' might be." Dave then opened up about smoking, drinking, being depressed, eating poorly, and leaving the track team. He desperately wanted to confide in his doctor as to why these changes had been happening, but his fear of rejection eventually won out and Dave kept his sexual feelings a secret. Instead, he just said he was having relationship problems, so his doctor recommended a counselor.

Dave knew that seeing a counselor would not help if he wasn't able to be out to his health providers. Because Dave knew he was definitely on the wrong health path, he went online and researched health issues that gay and bisexual people should discuss with their medical providers. He read that gay and bisexual people were at higher risk for mental health issues, smoking, substance abuse, and body image issues. What he found especially interesting was that those issues were more prevalent in people who remained in the closet and/or did not have adequate support services. Dave could totally relate to that and knew he had to get support. After working through some of his internal struggles with his counselor, Dave did come out in high school.

Soon after Dave publicly came out he began participating in the GSA group that Pat had started to give him the support he so desperately needed. In time, Dave was able to start taking better care of himself. He began exercising and he no longer felt the need to drink and smoke. Dave wished he could have been open to his pediatrician about his sexuality back in junior high, but doing so in that medical clinic didn't feel like a safe or welcoming place to come out.

Because of his experience, Dave promised himself that when he became a doctor, he would specialize in LGBTQ health issues and establish his clinic as welcoming to all. He was also thrilled to find, through online searches, listings of LGBTQ-friendly healthcare providers. He dreamed of the day he would be on those lists as a provider.

Hearing Dave's career dream was the impetus for Pat to go to college. He attended the undergraduate college in northeast Nebraska that Dave went to. They had a wonderful GSA student group. The school also welcomed frequent guest speakers on LGBTQ issues. During Pat's four years in college, he learned a lot about LGBTQ issues through my annual homecoming presentations, which gave him a better understanding about his gender identity. Pat majored in chemistry with hopes of one day getting a Ph.D. in the biosciences. By his senior year, Pat came to the realization that although he was born with anatomy consistent with the male gender, Pat actually identified internally as a female. What really resonated with Pat was the saying "sex is the body, but gender is the mind."

Armed with new, life-altering information and a renewed sense of self-identity, Pat came out as trans shortly before college graduation. Pat initially began to identify as gender queer and started using the pronoun "she" more in her own mind. She even toyed with the idea of going by the name of Veronica. Pat's brother, Dave, who by then was in medical school in St. Louis, was overwhelmingly supportive and encouraged Veronica to no longer hide what felt natural to her.

Veronica was accepted into a biomedical sciences graduate

program in Kansas City. She made a plan to begin transitioning to female while she worked to get her graduate degree. She couldn't think of a better place to start living her life openly and proudly. Although Veronica was not out to her parents about being trans, she was excited to attend school in an urban area where resources and support were more readily available.

Veronica's parents were thrilled with her decision to attend graduate school. It turned out that her mom's best friend from high school had a child named Lisa who would be moving to Missouri to attend medical school at the same University as Veronica. Shortly before student orientation, both moms insisted that their kids meet one another.

At their mothers' prodding, Veronica and Lisa finally did meet each other. Although Veronica wanted to talk to Lisa about her decision to transition, she was afraid the information might get back to her mother and Veronica just wasn't ready to deal with that quite yet. So Veronica introduced herself as Pat the first time she met Lisa. Fortunately, the two of them seemed to hit it off pretty well and they agreed to stay in contact during their time at school.

Lisa was a bright, intelligent woman who was born and raised in Utah. She was the oldest of four children and was raised in a strong religious community. It was not uncommon for the family to attend church and read passages from the bible together several times a week. Lisa studied hard in school because she'd always wanted to become a physician. During senior career day at her religious-based college, there were booths for several graduate schools, including a booth for a medical school in Missouri. Lisa had heard about this school through other pre-med classmates. She therefore applied to the Missouri medical school and was ecstatic when she was accepted.

During medical school orientation week, Lisa reviewed her class syllabus and read about my October presentations on LGBTQ healthcare. She had been taught that homosexuality was both a choice and a sin and therefore felt conflicted about learning about an "alternative lifestyle" in a medical school setting. Along with several other classmates, Lisa did not attend my October presentations, on the grounds that it was against her religious beliefs.

One afternoon, shortly after skipping my presentations, Lisa and several of her classmates visited a local doctor's office to shadow the primary care life of Dr. Xenart. During that afternoon, a new patient by the name of Veronica came in to see the doctor.

Veronica, who did not complete the intake paperwork sections about gender and sexual health, seemed visibly anxious and nervous as Dr. Xenart and his entourage of medical students paraded into the exam office. "I see that you did not complete the office paperwork," barked Dr. Xenart. Veronica slumped on the exam table, pondering whether to discuss her gender identity and her wish to start hormones. As she looked around the room of students, she became profoundly embarrassed upon locking eyes with Lisa, who immediately looked away in shock and dismay. Veronica had waited for weeks to finally obtain student health insurance and get in to see a doctor. But now she was seriously considering whether to further postpone her dream of transitioning.

Taking a deep breath, and with all the courage she could muster, Veronica said, "I was born with the anatomy of a male, but now I realize I am a female on the inside. I have felt this way for quite some time. I'd like to start taking hormones." Sighing with relief, Veronica was no longer slumping, because she had been able to openly and proudly state who she truly was to her new health care provider. Dr. Xenart's eyes popped out a bit as he was momentarily thrown off of his arrogant persona. His only response was, "Huh?" Veronica continued, "I just want my physical body to finally be the same as who I've always been on the inside."

At this point, Dr. Xenart regained his narcissistic air of superiority and exclaimed, "What are you talking about? You're a man. You don't get to choose your gender. God did that for you!"

Veronica turned pale as a ghost. She was speechless for a few seconds, hoping it was just a bad dream. It wasn't. Dr. Xenart said he was unable to help her, but he knew of a psychiatrist who could help her work through her "gender confusion." "Have you ever been treated for mental illness?" he asked in a demanding voice.

At that point, Veronica was horrified and embarrassed beyond belief. She politely allowed him to finish his tirade on "this transgender fad," as seen in the media, and further stated that he would consider it malpractice to treat her as any gender different than the anatomy she was born with.

Although Lisa did not attend my LGBTQ presentations earlier that week, she was appalled by the lack of knowledge and sensitivity demonstrated by Dr. Xenart. That evening, Lisa went home and researched trans people's experiences in doctor's offices. She was surprised to discover that Veronica's experience with Dr. Xenart was not uncommon. According to a national transgender discrimination survey, one out of every three trans people reported having negative experiences in a healthcare setting related to be trans, such as being assaulted, harassed, denied treatment, or having to teach their provider about trans care. What was of more concern for Lisa was that almost one-quarter of respondents didn't seek care when needed for fear of mistreatment [8].

Right then, Lisa made a commitment to be more open-minded and to attend all the presentations, including the ones on LGBTQ healthcare, regardless of her personal or religious beliefs. After all, someone Lisa knew was being impacted by prejudice and discrimination in a doctor's office.

Veronica, meanwhile, was devastated by her experience in Dr. Xenart's office and decided that it was not safe to come out about being trans.

As the months progressed, Veronica became increasingly depressed as she struggled with living away from home in a new state, as well as feeling she couldn't live openly as a female. As a way of self-medicating, Veronica began drinking almost daily to help calm her nerves and to help herself sleep.

She eventually turned to the Internet and discovered that there was a black healthcare market where people could obtain hormones.

She learned that many trans individuals had to resort to using the black market to obtain the hormones they need. This was due to the obstacles that many trans people face when it comes to receiving appropriate medical care. Since she didn't feel comfortable or safe seeking help from a licensed physician to get hormone management, Veronica began taking black-market estrogen. When she didn't get the results she'd hoped for, she doubled her dosage. Breast development began, but she also began gaining weight in other areas of her body. This weight gain was distressing to her.

Veronica thought there must be a better way to gain instant curves in the chest and buttocks areas. One day when she was walking in the LGBTQ-friendly part of town, she came across a flyer attached to a telephone pole stating, in big letters, "Pumping Party Tonight!" Veronica had heard about pumping parties as a quick way of getting instant curves, but until then hadn't known a way to access such services. She quickly called the number on the flyer to inquire.

"Bring $500 cash and come alone," she was told. She was given an address, which was a motel room for the one-night-only event. Although she was nervous and unsure of how the process would work, she was also ecstatic to finally be getting the curves she had always desired. She took out a cash advance from her credit card and went to the motel -- alone.

At the motel room, Veronica paid the $500 to the person at the door and was then offered the option of getting silicone injections into her breasts or buttocks. She was tired of waiting for the hormones to work, so she asked for both. She waited in line as she watched others lie down on the bed for the silicon injections. "Is this safe?" she asked the person who had taken her money at the door.

"Yeah. Jesse has been doing this for a long time and is known across the state for her expertise. You'll do great."

Then it was Veronica's turn. She was nervous, but also excited, as she laid down on the bed. She was hoping for the same positive response she had seen in the two women who'd gone before her. While receiving an injection in her buttock, Veronica experienced

severe pain that radiated down her leg. Shortly after, she began
having problems breathing and screamed out in pain and fear. She
couldn't breathe. Seconds felt like minutes. Before she knew it, the
once-full room was empty. Someone had called 911 as they fled the
room. An ambulance arrived and immediately rushed Veronica to the
emergency room.

Due to the severity of her condition, she was rushed to the coun-
ty's trauma center, where a team of medical providers were waiting,
including Lisa, who was doing her medical student rotation in emergency medicine that night. After she was assessed, she was found to
have an acute pulmonary embolism in addition to the nerve damage
from where the needle had been improperly inserted. Lab work
showed that Veronica had also developed hepatitis from when she
had shared dirty needles in the past, while injecting the hormones
she'd received off the black market.

Lisa discovered that the 911 caller had reported that Veronica
was having a bad reaction to a silicone injection. Her secret was out.

That night, Lisa went home and read about black market healthcare that some trans people receive, due to inadequate access to
competent trans care in the health community. She was shocked to
read that many trans people who receive their healthcare on the black
market can contract hepatitis or HIV through the use of shared
needles. An article in the *New York Times* [9] stated that up to 25%
of trans women reported having had silicone injections. Since
medical grade silicone can be hard to come by without hospital
connections, some unlicensed "pumpers" inject cooking oil or indus-
trial grade silicone, which is intended for cars and airplanes. Lisa also
read that silicone in the bloodstream can lead to acute breathing
problems, pulmonary embolism, connective tissues disorders, and
even death.

Even though Lisa was not part of the hospital inpatient service,
she visited Veronica twice a day to offer support and to discuss Veronica's experiences of receiving healthcare both through traditional
routes and on the black market. As Lisa listened and learned more

from Veronica about her experiences, she realized that Veronica did not choose to be trans, rather she was simply attempting to get her physical body to match how she felt on the inside.

Lisa's newfound knowledge about trans health, in time, grew into a passion to learn more. She went back to the medical school website and reviewed the online recordings of my LGBTQ health presentations. After her experience shadowing Dr. Xenart, Lisa was not surprised to hear in the recordings that many trans people have difficulty getting access to healthcare, due to lack of adequate coverage, as well as a lack of providers who are competent in addressing the social, cultural, and health issues that trans people face. She was saddened to learn that some trans people are at higher risk for drug and alcohol misuse, mental health issues, STDs, and complications from hormones and silicone. She also gained an appreciation for the importance of screening for cardiovascular health and certain types of cancers in the trans population [10].

Veronica stabilized medically over time and gratefully accepted the importance of being open and honest – not only with herself, but with her medical providers as well. With Lisa's help, and information from an online LGBTQ-provider search directory, Veronica found a culturally competent healthcare provider who welcomed her into his practice.

When Veronica was able to live her life openly and honestly, both to herself and to her doctor, she thrived medically and her depression and alcohol abuse resolved. She was finally on her way to the transition she'd been wanting.

Over the days of visiting Veronica during her hospitalization, Lisa realized that she had been wrong in judging LGBTQ people. She further realized that the Hippocratic oath she'd taken to "first do no harm" applied to everyone. She reflected back on the interaction Veronica had with Dr. Xenart and wondered if Veronica's near fatal experience after the silicone injection could have been avoided, if only she had been accepted for who she was on the day she attempted to come out to Dr. Xenart.

Because of that experience with Veronica, Lisa not only recommitted herself to treat all patients equally, but also decided to be an advocate for those in the healthcare system who tend to be marginalized, including people in the LGBTQ community. She joined her medical school's Advocates for Diversity in Medicine club and became a relentless advocate for all. Lisa even arranged for Veronica to be a trans advocate on a LGBTQ panel in front of her classmates, so that Veronica could share her story of trying to come out as trans to her doctor and, thereby, help ensure that future physicians would be better informed on the impacts they have on their future LGBTQ patients.

With time Veronica kept getting healthier and began thriving. She learned the importance of eating well, refraining from self-medicating, having appropriate medical and psychological screenings by her healthcare providers, and always being honest with her providers. It was clear to her that she'd been close to death because of the black-market silicone injection. Her courage to remain healthy and to be honest with her healthcare providers had never been greater.

Lisa and Veronica became close friends as the months progressed – just like their moms had been a quarter of a century earlier.

* * *

IF YOU ARE like Veronica and feel that you can't share information with your medical provider, please do whatever you need to find a provider with whom you can feel comfortable. Too many lives are lost because people have been afraid to share their real needs and their health stories with their medical providers. Don't let your story end because of that.

The support you need is available. There are culturally competent doctors who can provide the care you need and deserve who would welcome you into their practice. Keep looking and never give up. You deserve a life of health and happiness.

5

BULLYING

I WAS BULLIED and teased for many reasons throughout my child-hood and adolescence. Thinking back, I remember being picked on as early as grade school. I realize it is not uncommon to be picked on as a youth by other youths, and I was certainly not an exception.

When I was a kid, I often kept to myself during recess and stayed late after school, to avoid being picked on and challenged to fight. As I write this today, I can still remember the feeling of hiding in the school after the last bell had rung, waiting for the bullies to leave the building before I darted out the door to run home. It was not uncommon for me to sneak to the exit doors on the other side of the school as the bullies were waiting in vain for me by the doors most sixth graders left from.

On more than one occasion, my mom asked me why my clothes were full of snow when I came home from school. I didn't have the heart to tell her that I had been pushed down or had fallen while running away from my bullies. Even when she asked me point-blank if I was being picked on, most of the time I was too ashamed to be honest with her. It wasn't that I didn't want it to stop. The larger issue was that I didn't know things could be any better.

Actually, I'm not sure why I wanted to run home. I suppose it was because home is supposed to be safe. But my home wasn't safe, because I lived with the biggest bully of them all: my father.

Over time, a bullied person either develops a very thick skin or begins to have emotional and physical ailments as a result of their inability to cope with the continuous harassment.

In my opinion, there is nothing worse than being bullied by your own parent – for whatever reason. For as far back as I can remember, my father verbally tormented and bullied me, for numerous reasons, but most often for having what he called a big nose and for being gay. Although I didn't officially come out to my father until I was 23, that didn't prevent him from calling me names, including "fag." It was difficult enough growing up being anything outside of the norm in conservative Nebraska, but to be tormented about things I had not fully embraced, acknowledged in myself, and that I didn't have control over was the absolute worst.

Now that I am an adult, I realize that my father was most likely projecting his own insecurities onto me. I am certainly not condoning his behavior, but now I have a better understanding of what an insecure and cowardly man my father was. Some of you reading this may be getting bullied by your parent(s) or other important adults in your life, for whatever reason, and that is very painful. As children and teens, we always look for acceptance, encouragement, and validation from those we care about. Anything less than total acceptance can be painful, at best.

Bullying can be defined as *an attentive, determined, and premeditated hostile activity intended to harm, induce dread through the risk of aggression, and create pure terror.*

Identifying, acknowledging, and/or embracing sexual orientation or gender identity can be a lifelong process. Being seen as not conforming to society's expectations of gender identity, gender role, and sexual orientation can be a red flag for bullies. Sometimes, those who are struggling with their sexuality or gender identity themselves are the first ones to target others.

There is a good phrase I have heard, which I think is relevant here: *You are what you hate*. That phrase described me. I was so afraid of being outed I would often accuse others of being gay, just to take the heat off of myself. I mean, after all, why would a gay man tease or bully another man for being gay. Right?

That is a common projective defense mechanism that helps millions of people cope with feelings they can't accept in themselves. What I did was a good example of internalized homophobia. Homophobia may reveal itself in harassment, which can take the form of bullying – in person, online, or a combination of the two.

Many times, those who feel uncomfortable about their own insecurities are the first to point out those same issues in others. Sexuality and gender identity are no different. This does not mean that all people who tease and bully others about their sexual orientation or gender identity are gay or trans themselves, but it does mean that the bully may be struggling with those types of feelings, either within themselves or in someone close to them. If you think about it, why would someone else be so engaged in teasing someone about being gay or trans unless they were struggling with similar feelings themselves?

During my annual fall presentations at my alma mater in rural Nebraska, I have repeatedly seen the same students returning to hear me speak during all four years of their attendance at the school. I have seen, more than once, how the students most vocally against homosexuality in their freshman year end up coming out or becoming much more accepting by their senior year. I show compassion toward those students in the audience who are most vocal against being gay or trans, because I know that audience member may be one of the students who is struggling the most.

People often don't realize how revealing they truly are. I should know, because I used to be a bully myself. I identified with my father's bullying and became the aggressor, as a defensive measure. I would bully and tease others as a way of avoiding being bullied myself.

Much later in life, after I had grown up and accepted being gay, I was invited to attend the White House screening of the movie *Bully*. That was one of the most exciting times of my life. I loved meeting the Secretary of Education at the screening and was inspired by the courage of the *Bully* cast as they shared their stories after the screening. It's wonderful to see more awareness and education taking place about bullying.

I want to share a story with you about the many facets of bullying and being bullied.

Chris' Story

This is the story of a young person named Chris. I met Chris during one of my college presentations in northeast Nebraska. Chris graduated from a high school in suburban Chicago. It just so happened that Chris' high school teacher in Chicago, Tony, heard me at a presentation a decade earlier, when Tony had been a college student himself.

Tony had legally changed his name shortly after he graduated from college. Tony is trans and was teaching high school history in the suburb of Chicago where Chris grew up. Tony, who had taken Chris under his wing, reached out to me prior to Chris' enrollment in college. He let me know that Chris was going to start classes at the northeast Nebraska college, and asked if I would try to check in on Chris when I went back for my annual series of presentations in the fall.

Tony let me know that Chris was assigned as male at birth, but had grown up by identifying with both genders. He also let me know that Chris had become comfortable using the pronouns "they" instead of "he/she" and "their" instead of "his/her." I wrote Tony back to thank him for the introduction and assured him that I would be glad to connect with Chris when I was at the college.

What follows here is Chris' story. As you will see, I have chosen to use Chris' preferred pronouns. It is probably going to look a bit odd, and it may feel awkward to read at first; however, it's my hope that, as you encounter these pronouns over and over, you will become aware of how gendered our language and culture are. I am also hoping that, in this small way, you will gain an appreciation for what it's like for a young person who is gender nonconforming to live in our culture.

It's important to note that Chris' life journey may not be like anyone else's journey. That's an important point. Each of us is going to have experiences that are unique. And each one of us must do as much as we can to live our own story to the best of our ability.

I was thrilled to be able to meet Chris. Beaming with energy, they walked up and, without hesitation, gave me a big hug. In my experience over the years, freshman are often quite shy – but not Chris. I sensed that they had amazing strength and courage. Stereotypes were things that Chris seemed to have no use for. The notion that freshmen were shy was just another stereotype they seemed to be able to shrug off. We chatted for a while and they shared with me their story and how they ended up at that college.

Chris was the second child born to parents Maria and Jose. Chris had an older brother named Enrique who identified as a boy. All of Enrique's activities were rough and tumble. Maria would jokingly tell Chris and Enrique that if she had not been there the whole time, she would have thought they had come from completely different parents.

Maria was a strong Latina and an only child. Her parents had immigrated from Argentina when she was twelve years old. They came to America during a time of severe political unrest in Argentina. Her parents had been college professors when the government had cracked down on free thought. Maria's parents fled the country, eventually finding their way to Chicago, where they both became professors at the University of Chicago.

Maria had inherited a strong, free-thinking personality. Her parents – Chris' grandparents – felt a deep sense of pride as they watched their daughter grow into a fierce advocate for the underprivileged youth of inner-city Chicago. Maria was a social worker for a city agency when she met Jose. Jose was a young civil rights attorney who was trying to figure out how on earth he was going to make a living doing pro-bono work.

When he met Maria, Jose fell in love with all five-foot-two of the beautiful, young social worker. Maria was small in stature but a giant in strength and confidence. And those were traits she hoped to pass along to her children.

Enrique had no problem being the boss of the preschool. Those characteristics seemed to mature as part of his personality when he grew up. By the time he was in middle school, Jose and Maria had confidence that Enrique was going to navigate life just fine. However, regarding their second child, Chris, they found themselves less confident.

While Chris exuded confidence, just as Enrique did, Maria and Jose noticed some differences. As early as preschool, Chris showed an interest in both trucks and Barbie dolls. In first grade, during preparations for the church Sunday school production of the birth of Jesus, Chris protested the assigning of parts based on traditional gender roles and was eventually allowed to play the part of Mary, the mother of Jesus. At the time, most people thought it was cute that a little "boy" wanted to play the part of a "girl." But Maria and Jose shared a quiet heaviness for what might be ahead for their young child.

They continued to shower their youngest child with love and the space to develop in whatever ways Chris felt comfortable. Over time, Chris began asking if they could get a skirt like their best friend Jess wore. Maria didn't know quite what to do, but eventually decided to get Chris a red, kilt-like skirt. It wasn't exactly what little, ten-year-old Chris had in mind, but it was the start of what was to become one of the iconic fashion statements of Chris' life.

Chris encountered more and more challenges in school. The other kids were much less understanding than Chris' parents. Both Jose and Maria frequently found themselves in the role of educating the educators at Chris' elementary school. Fortunately, with some education from Chris' parents, the teachers and administrators did what they could to help Chris and the other children open their minds to gender role issues and gender nonconforming identities.

It wasn't easy for Chris, but they had the family traits of strength and determination, which included the view that challenges in life were thought of as adventures rather than obstacles. Over time, Chris seemed to almost embrace the reality that life was not going to be easy, but that being loved and supported made a huge difference. As Chris matured, they was able to defy any clear physical characterizations of gender. It was as if Chris embodied gender neutrality on all levels.

By the time high school rolled around, Jose and Maria had already scouted the faculty profiles of the high school teachers. They had picked out a teacher they hoped would be able to help their child navigate the new reality of high school. The teacher they identified was Tony Osborn. Tony openly identified as trans and was one of the faculty sponsors for the high school GSA group. In her not-so-subtle style, Maria contacted Tony by email a few weeks before school started and explained as much as she could about Chris. Tony was interested as much by Maria's passion as he was by Chris' story.

In the end, Tony did a lot to help Chris navigate high school. There were times when Chris would be wearing what had become their signature kilt-like skirt and would hear comments from other students. Some days, Chris would wear more generic or gender neutral clothing. Consciously or not, Chris was helping to expand awareness of gender roles in that suburban high school. Over time, most of the other students gained appreciation and understanding of what gender neutral identity was and how gender roles affect us.

As high school drew to a close, Chris was faced with questions about what to do next. By that time, Mr. Osborn had become Chris' go-to person for advice. When Tony had attended college in northeast Nebraska, he had not yet made the full transition from female to male, yet he had found the school to be quite helpful. He'd started to embrace the process of physical transition while he was a student there and had brought to attention the issue of bathroom issue for trans people.

Things actually went quite smoothly for Tony. The school administration instituted a clear policy stating that students were free to use whichever gender restroom they most identified with. Of course, there was the usual uproar among certain groups who cited the fears of male-to-female molestation when college-aged men used the women's room. Yet, as has been the case time and time again, there were no reports of trans people using the new policy as an excuse to molest anyone. Over time, most students forgot about it, and there were no reports of sexual misconduct as a result of a trans person using the restroom of their choice. Tony thought that this college might be a good place for Chris to check out.

Chris' parents were a little worried about their child traveling to such a rural area, but they had come to trust Tony's judgment. The clincher seemed to be when Chris toured the school and was able to have a one-on-one meeting with the chair of the theater department. Jose and Maria both agreed that maybe a small school like that would actually be the best place for Chris. So, Chris enrolled and anxiously awaited their move into a dorm and the start of a new journey in their life.

When freshman orientation rolled around, Chris couldn't have been more excited. They couldn't wait to meet the other freshman. Jose and Maria reluctantly said good-bye to their youngest child as Chris busily cleaned, unpacked, and settled into their dorm room. Their roommate had not yet arrived. All Chris knew was that the new roommate's name was Trevor.

About an hour after Jose and Maria bid farewell to Chris, Trevor and his parents came rolling onto campus. They were loud from the minute their fourteen-year-old Buick LaSabre, with its failing muffler, rolled into the parking lot. Chris could hear them as they ascended the stairs to the second floor of the dorm. Although the thought did flash through Chris' mind that this could be his room-mate, they quickly pushed that thought out of mind, thinking that there was no way God had that kind of twisted sense of humor. Well, much to Chris' chagrin, the next thing they knew, Trevor and his boisterous father rounded the doorway and dropped a load of boxes right in the middle of the room that Chris had just spent the last hour cleaning.

Trevor barely even smirked at Chris, did a quick fist-bump introduction, "Hey, I'm Trevor McDonnell and you're Chris?" Before Chris could say anything, Trevor had turned around to go retrieve more stuff from the LaSabre. Trevor's father, Bruce, on the other hand, instantly sensed that there was something a bit different about his son's new roommate. Bruce reached out and manhandled Chris' hand. He had a smile on his face, but, underneath the smiling veneer, Bruce looked more like a predator sizing up his prey. Trevor's mother, Lila, on the other hand, looked down at her worn-out sandals and studied her feet as if she'd just sprouted an extra toe.

It didn't take long for the McDonnell clan to transfer the contents of the LaSabre onto the middle of the dorm room floor. And then, barely even saying good-bye to their son, Trevor's parents rumbled away. Chris sat there, almost in shock. They would have stayed in a reverie had it not been for Trevor punching Chris on the shoulder and saying, "What do you say let's get out of here and go find us some beer and hook up with a few of those chicks down in the lobby?"

Chris, still reeling over the assigned roommate situation, blurted out a "No, go ahead, I'm fine here." Trevor said, "Fine. More for me then." And off he went. *Wow!* thought Chris, *What have I gotten myself into?*

That evening, Chris texted Jose and Maria while they drove back to Chicago. It was a lonely drive for them, as they were now officially empty-nesters. Chris, on the other hand, wished they was in the car with them instead of sitting in a dorm room dreading Trevor's return. Chris had managed to meet a few other freshmen that afternoon. While most people seemed nice, Chris did notice some puzzled looks as they looked them up and down.

As Chris drifted off to sleep that night, images of their parents driving back to Chicago came to mind, and then memories of high school and Mr. Osborn floated through their mind. Those comforting images helped Chris fall to sleep.

The next couple of weeks proved to be a whole new version of hell for Chris. Classes were going okay and they was managing to make a few more friends. Granted there were times that Chris would notice people looking at them in strange ways, and sometimes people murmured things under their breath, but Chis was used to that. Overall things were going OK - except when it came to things with Trevor.

Life in the dorm with Trevor was a challenge, even for someone as strong as Chris. Chris had talked to the Resident Assistant and to the head of student housing. A request for a room transfer had been made, but Chris had been told it could take a few weeks to months or more before a room might open up.

Chris knew Trevor could get into trouble with student housing because Trevor always kept their fridge stocked with Sierra Nevada Pale Ale. It seemed as if Trevor couldn't fall asleep unless he had at least a couple beers first. Chris chalked this up to the way Trevor had been raised. But it was against dorm rules to have alcohol on campus. Chris could have turned Trevor in, but they doubted it would accomplish much.

Chris returned to the dorm room one day to find Trevor holding up one of Chris' kilts. Trevor said, "What the hell is this? What kind of fag wears something like this?" Chris didn't respond at first. They had been down this road with bullies before. Then Chris channeled the five-year-old version of themself who had demanded to play the part of Mary in the Sunday School play. Chris calmly took the kilt out of Trevor's hand and said, "It's a kilt. I wear it and I'm proud to wear it. No matter how many times you call me a fag, I'm still going to wear it whenever I feel like it."

Trevor's eyes almost popped out of his head. "Whoa! You may be a fag, but you've sure got balls." Chris didn't even turn back around. They just plopped down on the bed, put in earphones, and acted like the two of them had just shared a pleasant conversation about the weather. They knew that feeding into Trevor's bullying behavior would only reinforce it.

Trevor stood there, mostly in shock. He struggled to reconnect with that bully persona that had kept him safe for so many years. But Trevor could feel something starting to crack inside himself. He felt a wave of tears coming up. Trevor flashed to images of his father verbally abusing his mother. He wanted to unleash all of his own pent-up rage onto Chris, but Chris didn't seem to be afraid of the attempts Trevor had made to intimidate them. Trevor was realizing that he didn't know what to do with that.

Almost a month went by and no alternative housing options had appeared for Chris. One day, in late September, Chris was on their way to psychology class, which was a class they shared with Trevor. It was the only class they had in common. On that day, there was a special lecture. It was the day I started presenting a series of lectures to the freshman psychology classes.

That was the day that Chris came up and gave me a warm hug right after the lecture. Chris didn't realize it, but Trevor was sitting in the back of the lecture hall, watching with curiosity as Chris exuded total confidence as they spoke with me.

Trevor's armor was definitely starting to crack. But it wasn't brute force that was causing the cracks; rather, it was the confidence and courage of his gender-nonconforming roommate that was slowly chipping away at Trevor's defensive walls.

Later that evening, Trevor burst into the dorm room after dinner, let out a deafening belch, and asked, "What's up lady-boy?" Trevor beamed as if he'd just invented a new language.

"Not much," replied Chris in their usual calm manner. Trevor bellowed, "Well, I thought that gay doctor guy was totally off today. What'd you think?" Chris calmly turned around and faced Trevor. They looked Trevor right in the eye and said, "I actually thought that part about bullying was pretty good."

"Say whaaaat?" said Trevor, as he tried to provoke Chris.

"Well, for starters, he talked about how people who have been bullied often bully other people. That was right on. He also said that bullies look for people who they think are weaker than themselves. And I agree with him that bullies themselves are often really frightened. He also said that bullying can take on many forms, like verbal, physical, isolating, intimidating, and sexual bullying. It all made a lot of sense to me," Chris said. "So I'm joining the PRIDE group and we're all going out to dinner with Dr. Holt tonight. We're going to talk about the support and resources that are available to those who are bullied. You wanna come along?"

"Uh...NO!" was all Trevor could come up with. And, with that, he walked out of the room. Chris could hear Trevor call out, "I'm going to go hang with some real men for a while. You and your gaaaaaay friends have fun at your gaaaaaay knitting party."

That night at dinner, Chris met some great people. There were other students in the PRIDE group, along with supportive faculty members and even some alumni of the group who came back every year. They had a great time and felt as if the year was finally starting to turn around.

On the way back to the dorm, Chris was chatting with a guy named Tim who was also a freshman. Tim was openly gay and was eager to learn about Chris' experience of gender queer identity. The two of them laughed and joked as they walked back to their dorms. Chris asked if Tim had met anyone to date. Tim giggled and pulled out his phone and opened up a gay dating app. Tim shared how it was pretty much a waste of time. "It's always the same people and they're not much fun. But last night I met someone I'd never seen on the app before."

Tim pulled up the guy's profile and showed Chris the pic of a guy that showed only his torso. Headless torso pics were not uncommon for people who were afraid of revealing their identity. Chris looked at the pic and said, "Nice abs." But then something besides six-pack abs caught Chris' eye. It was a six-pack, all right, and not the six-pack abs. In the background of the photo sat a six-pack of

Sierra Nevada Pale Ale. And the beer sat on a desk that looked hauntingly familiar.

Chris couldn't understand it. Trevor was the epitome of a homophobic, insecure, straight guy. There was no way the six-pack abs belonged to Trevor. Even so, Chris had to ask Tim, "So what was the guy's name?"

"I don't know for sure," said Tim. "He said it was Bob, but then later I thought I heard him tell me his name was Brent. Who cares. I've seen him around before, but I'm sure he's not out."

Chris really wanted to talk to Trevor that night to figure out what was going on, but Trevor was still out when Chris got back from dinner. Later that night, as they lay in bed, Chris couldn't shake the conversation they'd had with Tim. Finally, after an hour or two, Chris drifted off to sleep.

Unfortunately, sleep that morning was interrupted around 3:30 a.m., when Trevor came stumbling in drunk and turned on all the lights. Only when Chris awoke with a startle and instinctively cried out, "What the...!?" did Trevor have any inkling that maybe he should have been a bit quieter.

Chris watched as Trevor proceeded to more or less disrobe and flop onto his bed, all in one fluid motion. The lights were still on. Then a loud slurring expletive came out of Trevor. "I can't believe I left the damn lights on. Be a man for once and go turn 'em off for me."

After all that time they'd lived together, Chris was still shocked that Trevor would act that way. But, tonight, they decided to get out of bed and walk over to the light switch. Chris noticed that Trevor was giving them a more studied stare as they turned out the lights. "Thanks, homey," was Trevor's way of saying thank you.

After about 45 seconds of silence in the dark, Trevor blurted out, "So what *is* your problem? You're so weird. Just what *is* your problem?" Chris couldn't believe this conversation was happening, yet again. And at 3:30 in the morning.

Chris responded, "Nothing is wrong with me." But, this time, they decided to push in a different way and added, "What's wrong with *you?*" Chris held his breath and waited for an angry outburst. Instead, Trevor replied, "Sorry, dude, didn't mean for you to get your panties in a bind."

Chris could have let it go at that point – there it was, middle of the night – but instead of letting it go, Chris pushed just a bit more. "So, tell me more about your dad." They recalled the peculiar sense of predatory energy Trevor's father had given off the day they had met. "He's a jerk," Trevor replied. "What more do you want to know?"

"Well, tell me what's up with your parents," said Chris. "Your dad seems pretty intense and your mom seems really afraid for some reason."

It was pitch dark in the room, but Chris could sense that Trevor's demeanor had suddenly shifted. There was a faint crack in Trevor's voice as he said, "I couldn't wait to get out of that house. I've waited eighteen years to get out of there."

"Really?" asked Chris.

"Yeah, he's a jerk. My mom just puts up with it. She's afraid. We're all afraid of him. But I'm not afraid now."

The tension in the air was incredible. Chris knew something in Trevor was opening up, so they pressed on. "Sounds to me like you haven't always been all that strong."

Then... silence. It seemed like the silence went on for hours, although it was more like two or three minutes. Then Chris heard muffled sobbing across the room. Chris slowly sat up. Yes, they was sure now. Trevor was crying.

Chris didn't know quite what to do. They wanted to be rid of their bully roommate for weeks, yet now the bully was across the room weeping. They just sat there in silence for a while.

Finally, Chris lay back down and softly said, "It's okay, Trev. It's okay now. You're safe now. Nobody's going to hurt you anymore."

The next morning, Chris awoke before Trevor. Fortunately, Trevor's hangovers gave Chris plenty of time to shower and get out of the room before Trevor got up. Throughout the day, Chris kept replaying what had happened the night before. They knew that Trevor's wall had come down, but what they didn't know was whether or not the wall would come right back up.

Pretty soon, Chris got lost in the hectic schedule of his day. They was really looking forward to the public presentation that I was giving that day. Chris had learned at dinner the night before that we were going to be doing some experiential learning on the subjects of sexual orientation and gender identity. Even though the presentation was open to the general public and was not required for the students, Chris wasn't going to miss it.

By the time Chris got to class, they hadn't seen Trevor all day. They was a little bit worried about him, but tried not to let their thoughts interfere with the presentation. It was an incredible presentation. We did an experiential exercise where people learned that gender identity flows along a spectrum, just as sexual orientation does. Thinking of gender in binary terms labeling people as only male or only female reduces the complexity and beauty of what it means to be human.

In my experience, freshman are usually the shy ones in the back of the room. Chris was the first freshman I had seen who volunteered to tell their personal story in front of a room full of strangers. As Chris spoke, I was reminded of a younger, pre-transitioned Tony from several years earlier. Chris seemed to have taken all that Tony had taught them, and was taking it to the next level.

Chris shared great information with the group about what it was like to be gender queer. As Chris spoke, they felt alive as never before. They had found a calling. It was as if the universe had set everything in motion to lead up to that one moment.

As their presentation came to a close, the audience sat in silence. Some were weeping, some were sitting there feeling shocked from the story. As people started to slowly leave the lecture hall, Chris caught a glimpse of an older woman who looked vaguely familiar. They couldn't place who she was right away, but then it hit them. It was the woman who had been looking down at her feet the day Trevor moved in. It was Trevor's mom, Lila!

As Chris walked back to the dorm late that afternoon, they had too many thoughts and confusing feelings swirling around. Was that actually Trevor's photo on the gay dating app? Would Trevor's angry bullying personality come raging back after last night's conversation between them? And what was Trevor's mom even doing at one of Dr. Holt's presentations?

When Chris arrived back at the dorm, they stood outside the room for a minute, then took a deep breath, put the key in the lock and opened the door. *Whew!* The room was empty.

Chis looked around, feeling a little worried about Trevor. Then they noticed a note on the mirror. It read "I'm out for the night, back whenever." *Okay*, thought Chris. *Well, at least Trev's still alive.* They couldn't believe they'd even had that thought.

The rest of the evening went okay. It was actually nice for Chris to have the room to themself that night. They could finally get some studying done, and they even had time to Skype with their parents in Chicago.

When Chris went to bed that night, they knew that sooner or later they'd have to face Trevor again. It bothered them that they had no clue how Trevor might react. Maybe he would act like they'd never had the conversation. Even so, Chris wondered about that gay app pic and about Trevor's mother's presence at Dr. Holt's lecture. Chris was eager to figure those things out, but it probably wouldn't happen anytime soon.

It was a crisp evening. The smell of autumn was in the air. Chris was feeling more at home in their rather strange living arrangement. Depending on how Trevor and they navigated things around their conversation from last night, maybe they would remain in this dorm room after all. In spite of being more primal than domesticated, Trevor did seem to have something deep inside that was decent. If only he could really let down all those walls he'd built up. With that thought, Chris drifted off to sleep.

Around 2:30 in the morning, they was awakened by a pounding on the door. Chris' heart almost leaped out of their chest. They scrambled to the door, not knowing what to expect. They cracked the door, just a bit. It was Trevor.

Chris threw the door open. "Why are you knocking!?"

"I can't get my keys out of my damn pocket" slurred Trevor as he stumbled into the room. He flopped down on his bed and started talking about how much fun he'd had that night. There had been lots of hot girls and lots of alcohol for everyone.

Chris thought about things for a moment and then guessed that if Trevor was, indeed, as drunk as he seemed, they might be able to get some information out of him that he might not otherwise be willing to share. So, very carefully, Chris decided to circle around and work the conversation toward the gay dating app issue.

Chris started by asking about the women who had been at the party. "So, there were hot girls at the party?"

"Yeah, way more than you'd know what do with. Well, not *you*, but more than...." His words trailed off in a slurred decrescendo.

Chris could have let it drop then, but decided to try again. "So, did you have sex with any of them?"

No response. Chris looked over at Trevor. It looked like he'd passed out. Chris got up and said, "It's just as well, given what you told me about your dad last night. You're better off drowning your miseries, if you can."

With that, Chris got up and went into the bathroom to get a drink of water. They drank the water and then looked into the mirror at their reflection staring back. What were these feelings they was having? Chris realized they was starting to feel something different toward Trevor.

Chris shrugged their shoulders and, just as they turned around to flip off the light they gasped, and jumped into the air. There stood Trevor. He was blocking the doorway. Chris was about six inches shorter than Trevor, so they ducked down to pass underneath Trevor's outstretched arm that was blocking the doorway.

Trevor instantly moved to block Chris' attempt to get past him. "C'mon Trev," Chris said. "It's late. I don't have time for this."

No response from Trevor. Chris felt a lump in their throat. "What's going on?" said Chris, as they stood up straight and looked Trevor in the eyes. All Chris could hear was the pounding of their heart and they started to panic. Trevor still said nothing.

More panic. Was Trevor going down the very same path of abuse that his father had gone down? Chris recalled the Skype call with their parents earlier that evening. *At least my parents will know I loved them*, Chris thought.

Then Trevor looked right into Chris' eyes and, with a steel-cold stare, said, "No, I didn't have sex with any of those girls. And, yes, I heard everything you said – last night *and* tonight."

Chris gulped. *This is it*, they thought. *Think fast.*

Right when Chris was ready to try again to dart past Trevor and run into the hallway, Trevor grabbed Chris by the shoulders and, from inches away, hissed the words, "I am not my father. I'm different from him." There were a few tense seconds that felt like hours. Here it was 2:30 in the morning and after months of tension, these two very different roommates were finally facing off. And then in the next instant, Trevor pulled Chris toward him. And he kissed them.

"What the...?!" exclaimed Chris. "What are you doing, Trev?" They broke loose and scrambled past Trevor.

Trevor stood frozen. Then he slowly turned and said, "I don't know what's going on inside me. I know I'm an idiot sometimes – well, okay, most of the time. Anyway, you're different. And not because of those damn skirts you wear. You're different because you're way stronger than me *or* my dad. You have the courage to be you. And to let other people be themselves." Trevor looked down, tears welling up in his eyes. "I don't just admire you, Chris. I love you."

Chris couldn't help it. They walked back over to Trevor and hugged him. They stood there in a powerful embrace. Each wept their own tears, as they had both done before, many times, but this time they wept with each other. Two very unlikely spirits had found each other.

Over the next few weeks, Trevor and Chris tried to sort out their feelings. Trevor certainly had a lot of sorting to do. He struggled with labels. What did it mean that he loved a gender-queer person? Did that mean he was gay? He had tried to date a guy he'd met on the gay dating app. Chris learned that it was, indeed, Trevor who had hooked up with Tim that night. But Trevor really didn't enjoy being with Tim. Trevor had also been with lots of women, but he'd never had feelings for anyone like he was having for Chris.

In the end, Chris helped Trevor move beyond his need for labels. "Love is love is love," Chris would say. "Let other people worry about the labels. We'll just call it what it is – love." That resonated with Trevor. He was growing in ways he'd never imagined possible.

Chris, on the other hand, had to sort out what it meant to go down a path of dating someone who had so clearly been a bully. Over the next several weeks, Trevor's hard exterior melted more and more. He cut way down on his alcohol intake, and Chris helped him see that real strength wasn't gained from putting other people down. Trevor was learning from Chris that real strength comes from embracing all that you are and then living that true self fully and completely.

Thanksgiving was around the corner. Trevor asked Chris to go home with him for Thanksgiving. Trevor had taken to referring to his parents as "Bruce" and "Lila," in part to symbolize his maturation and remind himself that he was no longer under their house rules.

Chris had not talked to Trevor's parents since the day they had dropped Trevor off at school. They wasn't too sure Bruce and Lila would be okay with their son dating someone who didn't fit into the limited categories it seemed that they had always known and wanted for Trevor.

But Chris decided to give it a try. If it didn't work out, they would only be an hour away from the school and could easily go back to the dorm. Besides, Chris was still curious about why Trevor's mom had been at Dr. Holt's lecture that day. Chris had asked Trevor about it, but Trevor completely dismissed it as unlikely, saying that Chris was probably mistaken. After all, there was no way his mother would drive an hour to go to a presentation like *that*.

On Thanksgiving morning, Chris and Trevor arrived at Bruce and Lila's home. Lila was thrilled to meet the new "special person" in her son's life. Trevor was learning how to communicate without relying on gendered pronouns as much.

When Trevor and Chris stepped out of the car, Lila and Bruce came out of the house to greet them. However, Lila froze in her steps, and a chill descended upon the moment, as Bruce and Lila watched Trevor put his arm around Chris.

Lila was speechless. Bruce glared at Chris, and then Trevor. "You don't need to introduce me to that faggot roommate of yours. I know what the hell is going on. I should have known you'd turn all girly on us when we left you in that dorm room with that thing you call a roommate of yours," spat Bruce. With the hatred still spewing out of him, Bruce turned and walked back inside the house, slamming the door.

Lila regained her composure, stepped forward and touched Trevor's shoulder as she said, "It's so good to see you, son. Please don't mind your father. You know how he gets."

Chris couldn't believe what had just happened. But they decided that this was Trevor's battle to fight. They would stand at Trevor's side, but Trevor was going to have to sort this one out.

The three of them walked inside, passing by Bruce who was guzzling a can of beer as he watched a football game on the big-screen TV. Lila, Trevor, and Chris went into the kitchen and made small talk as Lila finished preparing the Thanksgiving dinner.

When it came time to eat, Lila had Chris and Trevor sit down and then called out to Bruce, "Dinner is ready, Honey. Do you want to come in?" It was as if Bruce had been waiting for that moment to have a reason to explode. He threw his half-empty beer can at the living room wall and walked into the dining room. "I ain't eating with no faggots. It's bad enough that my son lives in a dorm with one, but I'm not sitting here like it's okay. God says it's a sin and I believe what God says." He turned to walk back into the living room.

Trevor stood up. "Dad. Get in here. Now," Trevor said calmly. "We've come here today to be with you and Mom. If you want to be a jerk, then wait until we're gone."

Silence. Then it seemed that the *tick-tock-tick-tock* of the heirloom grandfather clock grew louder. *Tick. Tock.* Time had slowed to a crawl.

Bruce turned around. The veins in his forehead pounded as his furrowed brow and cold green eyes locked onto Trevor. He took one step forward. Then another. Moving slowly, deliberately. Clenching his teeth and his fists as he moved closer. He was just inches from Trevor.

At the last moment, Lila stepped between Trevor and Bruce. She pleaded, "Please boys, let's just sit down and eat dinner and then...." Before she could finish, Bruce reached out and shoved her away. That was the last straw for Trevor. He reached deep inside himself. He had never stood up to his father before, but this was going to be the last time he stood by while his father abused someone.

Just as Trevor was ready to attack Bruce, Lila screamed, "Stop it! Enough! Enough! Both of you sit down right now!" Lila had never asserted herself like that before. Both Trevor and Bruce froze, not so much out of fear, but out of shock. Here was this timid, verbally abused woman who was now screaming at the top of her lungs.

"SIT DOWN!" She screamed again. "I SAID, 'SIT DOWN!'"

Trevor, Chris, and even Bruce all sat down. "Enough!" screamed Lila. "Enough! This has to stop! And it has to stop now! Bruce, I've put up with your abuse all these years. It ends today. Today the truth is coming out." At that point, there was a noticeable shift in Bruce. It was as if his rage began to crumble.

Lila continued, "Trevor, you know that I love you. I love you no matter who you love. And, Chris, if Trevor loves you, then that's good enough for me. I love you, too, and you're welcome in our home anytime."

Lila's focus turned to her husband. Tears streamed down her cheeks as she said, "Bruce. I've put up with your abuse all these years. You've been a miserable man and you've taken your anger out on me. That is not going to happen ever again. I know about you, Bruce. I've always known about you. You didn't think I knew, but I did."

Trevor and Chris exchanged puzzled looks. Then they noticed what was happening to Bruce. It was almost as if Bruce started to melt. He slouched in his chair. He looked down.

Lila said, "Bruce, I've known all these years. I finally had the nerve to go hear a psychiatric doctor give a talk at Trevor's college a couple of months ago. I learned how bullying works. You've used your power as the head of this household to beat us down, thinking we couldn't fight you back. You have terrorized us."

She stood up straighter. "I finally found the words to know who you are. I know you've been going to Sioux City to that gay bar. I know you love women, but I also know you've loved men. I didn't understand how that could be until that presentation at the college. I've known about you, but you were always so afraid. It's one thing if you can't face the truth in yourself, but it's another thing entirely when you take it out on my son. Trevor is a good man, and it looks like he's happy with Chris. I ain't gonna let you destroy them just because you can't face yourself. It's time you faced the truth and quit lying. Quit lying to us all."

Silence. Dead silence.

At that point, in almost a whisper, Lila said, "I learned at that presentation, Bruce, that in order for me to heal, I gotta let go of this anger I have for the way you have bullied us. So, Bruce... I forgive you, but your bullying *is* gonna stop."

Then Bruce let out a slight muffled cry, followed by a definite cry, which grew into full-on sobbing. Soon Bruce was wailing. All the walls he'd built up to protect himself came tumbling down. All the years of hiding in fear were coming to an end.

Needless to say, the turkey never made it to the dining room table that day. The drama trumped the turkey. Instead, they had turkey sandwiches later that night as they each started to embrace the truth.

On that Thanksgiving Day, Trevor's family found something to truly be grateful for. Each one, in their own way, had outgrown the labels and definitions that had been slowly killing them. As a result of their encounter with a confident, young, gender-nonconforming student, they all found the courage to be true to themselves. They would each, ultimately, go on to live the lives they were always meant to live.

The bullying in Trevor's family went into permanent hiatus when they learned what Chris had to teach them. They learned that true strength doesn't come from putting other people down. True strength comes when you accept who you are.

* * *

PLEASE KEEP IN MIND, just as Chris did, that the person who is bullying you is placing their own insecurities onto you. If you think about it, the only reason someone would pick on another is that they can't tolerate their own feelings. You don't have to carry their issues for them. If you can't be accepted for who you are, you are better off without them.

If you are being bullied, it's really important to find supportive people you can talk to, and to connect with like-minded people, such as in a group or a club at school. It can really help to find support and self-worth outside of the home if your home environment is not healthy. That may include reaching out to neighbors, school counselors, teachers, relatives, or other important figures in your life and asking for help and support around being who you are.

6

COMING TOGETHER

Two issues that some LGBTQ people struggle with the most are low self-acceptance and low self-esteem. LGBTQ people are not born feeling bad about themselves. Low self-worth is often a result of prejudice, rejection, discrimination, and victimization. Even if a child is born into a very supportive home environment, a continuous hostile societal environment can continuously assault a person's sense of self-worth.

When I was growing up, I struggled tremendously with my self-esteem. I could do nothing right in the eyes of my father, which left me second-guessing myself constantly. I felt that no matter how hard I tried, I just wouldn't ever be good enough. I struggled greatly with accepting who I was, which was complicated by the continuous harassment by my father. Every day, he would sit me down and lecture and berate me. My father told me I was not meeting his expectations and that I should be someone other than who I was. There is no question that his consistent and abusive behavior took its toll on me.

Growing up as a closeted gay male in Nebraska was a challenge that involved not only attempting to stay out of trouble with my father, but also coming to grips with my sexuality. Each time my father got angry, which was daily, he would go on tirades criticizing and judging people. It was the gay-bashing comments that left the biggest emotional scars.

As children, we are always looking for approval from our parents. When we feel we are not accepted for who we are, we are left with feelings of guilt or shame.

The good news is that self-esteem can be enhanced by a loving environment. When you are young, you look to any parental figure for approval. This figure may or may not be your parents. It may be necessary for you to find support and acceptance outside of your home.

A supportive community may include neighbors, school counselors, teachers, or other important figures in your life. If you find yourself struggling with low self-esteem and self-acceptance, it is important to surround yourself with like-minded people. Being surrounded by friends   one-on-one or in a group at school – can provide support and comfort.

Self-acceptance can only come when you grow to love yourself for who you are. It is important to remember that you cannot be all things to all people. No matter what, you are not going to be able to please everyone all of the time. In fact, it can be emotionally unhealthy to strive to be loved and accepted by everyone.

Not being able to be true to yourself can lead to significant emotional consequences, including shame or guilt over not being "perfect". No matter who you are or what you stand for, you deserve unconditional love and acceptance. If you feel you don't fit in with your current group of friends or acquaintances, then it's time to move on to find others. The important thing is that you surround yourself with people who value and accept you for being you.

I suffered from depression, anxiety, and, on occasion, thoughts of suicide, starting from when I was in high school. Trying to live my life to be liked and accepted as someone I was not was painfully difficult. Being unable to be true to myself made me feel isolated, scared, and frightened to be close to others. I was afraid that being close to others would result in being discovered as someone "outside the norm." And that felt dangerous. Even if others knew when I was young that I was gay, I didn't have the capacity then to tolerate such knowledge of myself. I hid in extracurricular activities at school and attempted to excel in anything that gave me the feeling of being accepted.

It wasn't until I began my own therapy and found a supportive group of friends that I was able to be true to myself and develop a healthy sense of self-worth. I wish organizations like GLSEN (Gay, Lesbian, and Straight Education Network), GSAs, and the Trevor Project had been available when I was struggling with my self-esteem as a youth. It would have made my self-acceptance and self-love much easier to achieve.

In this final main chapter, I want to share how the characters I've introduced in the stories came to embrace their true, authentic selves.

Together as One

In this book, you have traveled alongside several students whose stories I have created. But there is more to each of those stories. As I said earlier, every year I travel back to my alma mater college in northeast Nebraska, where I give presentations about LGBTQ issues. Over the years, I have watched many young people transform themselves from frightened freshman to shining, confident leaders in the work for LGBTQ equality.

This particular college in Nebraska has a strong PRIDE Group. Every year, during homecoming week, current and former PRIDE members and supportive staff and faculty all gather for a luncheon. There is a lot of activity during homecoming week, with the PRIDE luncheon always held on the day of the homecoming football game. The college's president, and other faculty members, frequently make a point of dropping by the luncheon to show their support for the PRIDE students. Needless to say, the room is always buzzing with energy.

The following is a story of one of those luncheons.

When we last left Jim, he had sent off his love letter email to Mark. It was Jim's first love letter that he sent. The only problem was that Jim and Mark were like two different species. Jim was slowly working his way out of his protective shell, while Mark had made tons of friends at college. Given that their worlds were so vastly different, Mark and Jim had barely spoken to one another since they had arrived on campus.

Jim often quietly watched Mark in the distance when they were both in the dining hall. Mark would be off in the southwest corner, eating with the rest of the baseball players. Jim had labeled them the "baseball bros." Even though Mark was a freshman, it was as if he'd already fully assimilated into the role of an up and coming star collegiate athlete.

Jim had sent the email to Mark on a Wednesday. It was now Saturday, and he was feeling some regret. Jim was beginning to retreat back into his familiar shell of shame. He thought to himself, *How could I have been so stupid to have sent that email to someone? And not just someone, but a someone who is Mark!*

Jim tried to block the whole thing out of his mind. Since he had memorized Mark's schedule, and memorized it even better than Mark had, Jim reasoned that he would be able to avoid Mark completely.

During my lectures that week, Jim heard me talk about the PRIDE group. He decided it would be good for him to look into it. When he spoke with the faculty advisor, Tracy, he said he wanted to meet some other LGBTQ students. Tracy had explained that the PRIDE group could help with the tools he needed for self-acceptance and growth – tools such as access to community support, strong connections with friends and faculty members, positive role models, school safety, support networks, and the development of healthy coping strategies. Jim was impressed and felt as if the group could offer him a safe place where he could feel welcomed. Besides, it might help take his mind off of Mark.

Jim decided to attend the PRIDE luncheon, which seemed like perfect timing being it was just days after emailing Mark. All the other students seemed to be having fun with their friends. So, Jim pulled together all the courage he could find and left the safety of his dorm room to find out where the PRIDE luncheon was being held.

Tracy had told him the luncheon would be held in one of the VIP rooms at the Student Center, but he had forgotten the exact directions that Tracy had given him. When he finally made it to the student center, he set about trying to locate the room. Searching for the right room in the Student Center, he felt like a rat in a maze. He went down one hallway after another, poking his head into rooms full of happy, laughing alumni and students. All the rooms were filled with people attending the various reunions taking place on homecoming weekend. Room after room of loud laughter and warm hugs. Jim felt more alone with each step as he went down one hall after another.

He was just about to give up and go back to his dorm room when he saw a sign directing people to the PRIDE luncheon. He breathed a sigh of relief and turned the corner to go down that hallway. He could see a sign for the PRIDE group toward the end of the hallway. Between where he was and that sign, there were lots of people standing in the hallway attending other reunions. They were greeting and embracing each other. They barely noticed a timid freshman quickly walking down the hallway. Jim was almost ready to start running toward the room, just so he could duck in and escape all the chaos.

Finally, as Jim neared the PRIDE luncheon room, he stopped. No, he froze in his tracks. There, not more than ten feet away, between him and the room where the luncheon was being held, stood the baseball players, "the baseball bros." And, in the middle of that group, with his back toward Jim, was Mark.

Jim stood paralyzed. *What am I going to do now?* His thoughts were racing. *Do I turn around and go back? No. I've come this far.*

Turning around now is turning away from myself. I've come too far in my life. This luncheon is too important to miss.

Jim glanced at the group of baseball studs, who were not looking at him. *Of course they haven't noticed me! I'll just sneak past them and dart into the luncheon. Mark will never even see me.*

With that, Jim put his head down and plunged the final twenty feet of his journey to escape into the luncheon. Just as he was almost past the "baseball bros," he heard Mark's voice, the voice Jim had played out a million times in his mind – *that* voice, calling his name. All of Jim's fantasies of himself and Mark included Mark gently calling his name. This time, however, it was for real. Jim heard Mark say, "Hey Jim."

Jim froze, again. His heart stopped. *Oh No! I can't possibly face this kind of embarrassment.*

But it was too late for Jim. He had been spotted by the stud athlete who had, only days before, received Jim's love letter.

Jim swallowed a huge lump in his throat and looked up. There stood Mark. The rest of the baseball guys fell silent. Jim was silent. Mark was silent.

Then Mark turned to the bros and did the fist-bump-shoulder-bro-hug thing. He said, "Thanks guys, I'll see ya tomorrow." The rest of the guys stood back a bit as Mark emerged from the center of the group.

There stood Jim, still frozen, turning a deeper and deeper shade of red as each second felt like an eternity. Jim gathered his courage again and looked up, looked directly at Mark. Mark's face had an expression that looked to Jim like a faint grimace. Mark said, "I got your email. I told the guys about it."

This is it! I'm dead! Jim's eyes darted, trying to find the fastest exit out of there. Before his trembling legs could figure out what to do, Mark took a step closer. Jim looked up. *Gulp.*

Mark opened his arms, reached out, and powerfully grabbed Jim into an embrace that could have ended all embraces. Jim instantly started to cry. Jim was crying, but right there in his arms was Mark. And, yes, Mark was crying too. Jim realized he was not alone.

The baseball bros all quietly took a few more steps back. A couple of them fought off tears of their own. Then they turned and walked away. There stood Mark, embracing Jim. By then they both had tears streaming down their cheeks.

Their embrace was more powerful than Jim had ever imagined it could be. Time was frozen, but warmth and love was embracing the two of them as they stood there holding each other.

Finally, Mark raised his tear-soaked eyes off of Jim's shoulder. He gently kissed Jim's neck and whispered, "Thank you for your email." With that, they turned and walked into the PRIDE luncheon together.

Inside the luncheon, there were people of all sizes, ethnicities, ages, and positions within the college. People were standing around talking as Jim and Mark walked in. Neither of them had ever really met another openly gay person before. They found themselves surrounded by other LGBTQ students, alumni, and supportive faculty members.

Mark couldn't believe it – there was his chemistry professor, Dr. Russell!

Dr. Russell and his wife had been amazing mentors to me, starting when I had been a student. The three of us stood talking together and sharing warm memories. Dr. Russell was pointing out how the figure of the college mascot, a Wildcat, on the ice-cream cake was drawn in an anatomically incorrect way. "No, we are not talking about genitalia here," Dr. Russell said, and pointed out that there were five toes on the paw, and Wildcats only have four toes.

Mark and Jim shifted their focus to another part of the room and saw several other professors. One of them was Dr. Tim, from the psychology department, and there were several professors from the education department, including Dr. Lenny. They all recognized Jim and Mark and greeted them with warm smiles.

Jim recalled from my talk how influential Dr. Tim had been to my husband when he was a student at the college. In one of the presentations, I had shared how Dr. Tim, in his relaxed, non-lecturing style, had been a significant influence during my husband's spiritual and professional journey. Jim was starting to see that education involved far more than sitting in a lecture hall taking in bits of information. Education, he realized, was about transformation. He was right. Education is about transformation of the heart and soul.

Jim turned his attention to another part of the room. He couldn't believe his eyes when he saw that the college president was in the room. Jim had just passed probably twenty or more rooms of alumni, college trustees, and dignitaries in the other rooms. But, here at the PRIDE luncheon, stood all of these professors and the president. *Wow!*, thought Jim. *Back home, people told me I was a sinner and a pervert, but here are all these professors, and even the college president, and they're all showing their support for people like me!* Jim felt a deep sense of pride and the encouragement to be himself.

Jim's reverie was soon interrupted, as a distinguished and loving woman with white hair approached. She opened her arms and embraced Jim and Mark, in turn. It was Tracy – the faculty advisor of the PRIDE group. "I'm so glad you both were able to make it today." This was the Tracy that Jim and Mark had both, independently, reached out to only days before. She had encouraged both of them to attend this luncheon. And here they were.

Soon, it was time for the program to get started. Jim and Mark scrambled to find seats at a table. It reminded Jim of musical chairs. He searched frantically to find a place to sit. Before he could figure things out, Mark gently pulled at his hand to go sit with a young woman who was gesturing for them to sit by her. The woman had been talking with the college president. Jim and Mark assumed she must be some sort of dignitary with the school, even though she looked to be about their age.

Mark and Jim walked over and sat down. They were at a table in a corner of the room and Jim felt relieved. After the wild morning he had just experienced, he was glad to sit down at the edge of things.

He selected a seat with his back to the rest of the room and the doorway. He just wanted to close off a bit and collect his thoughts. Jim was sitting next to Mark and could focus his attention on Mark and the kind woman who had invited them over.

The young woman extended her hand to the guys, full of confidence, her eyes beaming with warmth and love. "Hi, I'm Bria," she said.

Jim and Mark introduced themselves, and instantly felt as if they had known Bria all their lives. It was almost impossible not to feel comfortable around Bria. Jim and Mark were impressed with her amazing personality. She was strong and not easily intimidated, yet she was also beautifully gentle.

They asked her if she worked with the college president. "No, not yet," she replied, with a twinkle in her eye. Bria shared with Mark and Jim the details of her life over the past couple of years. They both sat almost in a trance as Bria described what she had been through. Jim could relate to Bria's story and the despair she described.

Given Bria's remarkable strength and confidence, Jim imagined that Bria was a junior or, more likely, a senior at the college. He noted her familiarity with the faculty and, particularly, the way she'd confidently spoken with the college president. Jim was rapidly becoming an admirer of the young woman's strength and courage. He thought to himself, *I want to learn from her. I want to be as strong and confident as she is when I'm a junior or senior.*

Finally, Mark asked Bria, "So what's your major?"

"Pre-law."

"I can totally see you in the courtroom. Have you been accepted to a law school yet?" Mark asked.

Bria chuckled. "No, you don't apply to law school until after you've taken the LSAT in the summer of your junior year."

"Ah," said Mark. "So I suppose you're busy studying for it now?"

Again, Bria just chuckled. She looked up at the guys and said, "No, I'm a freshman, just like you two."

They almost fell out of their seats. The day was full of surprises.

The three of them spent the rest of the luncheon laughing and sharing stories. There they were, each with such different backgrounds, yet the PRIDE luncheon had brought them together. They were developing the bonds that could well become the start of life-long friendships.

The food was served, and people joked and laughed together. It was shaping up to be a family gathering if ever there was one.

When lunch was finished, I asked everyone to go around and introduce themselves. Then I announced that I had invited some alumni to come back today and give short talks on how the PRIDE group had helped them when they were in college.

I told the audience how the first two speakers had met eight years earlier as freshmen. They had been together in a relationship since their freshman year, and were now graduate students in New York. I introduced them by saying, "Please welcome Chris and Trevor."

Chris and Trevor talked about how they had met and how their relationship had powerfully transformed Trevor's understanding of gender, his family's dynamics, and his relationships with his parents. Trevor shared that he was working on his doctorate in gender studies.

Trevor also shared with the group some of the details of his journey since he and Chris had met. He described how Chris had been a powerful example to him of how to live life courageously every day. Trevor described how his relationship with Chris had affected and changed his parents' lives. Trevor's parents had divorced several years ago. His mother, Lila, was now a junior in college and was planning to get her elementary school teaching degree. She had been involved in starting a PFLAG chapter in the small town where Trevor had grown up. Trevor gave a shout out to Lila, who was there at the PRIDE luncheon.

Lila came up and discussed how she loved PFLAG's advocacy and education for families and friends of the LGBTQ community.

Trevor's father, Bruce, had moved to Tulsa, Oklahoma, where he was working as a counselor for men who had been convicted of the crime of domestic violence. He was helping men break down the walls that had led to their abusive violence toward others.

Chris was in a graduate program in theater. They described how their four years at college had been both amazing and eye-opening. They said that the undergraduate theater program had given them a vision of how to expand human consciousness on stage and how to use drama to tell stories that could break down the walls we construct around gender and gender roles.

I introduced another alumnus by sharing how I had met Veronica several years ago and how she had emerged to be a regional leader in trans healthcare issues.

Veronica shared with the group about her struggle to find appropriate healthcare. She became tearful as she explained that, had it not been for the persistence of a young physician, she might have ended up a casualty of botched medical care. However, because of her "knight in the white lab coat," as Veronica referred to that doctor, she had managed to get the appropriate healthcare she needed.

Then Veronica introduced her "knight in the white lab coat," who had traveled with her to attend the luncheon. She introduced "Dr. Lisa." I instantly recognized Lisa from several years ago when she was a first-year medical student. Lisa and Veronica shared how they had collaborated over the years, working to facilitate better care in the lives of many transgender people who were trying to navigate the healthcare maze.

Just as the luncheon program was about to end, a woman who looked to be in her mid-forties walked in. She seemed a little out of place because she didn't appear to be an alumnus or a student.

Tracy walked over to greet the woman. "Welcome. Can I help you?"

"I'm Alice," the woman said, "I've been standing outside listening. I've really been wanting to connect with a group like this, because I've felt moved to start a PFLAG chapter in my town. I heard Dr. Holt talk earlier this week and now I'm ready to do what I can to help young people and their families in my town. I just wanted to meet some of you and say hello. I hope that's okay."

Tracy spent the rest of the time visiting with Alice as the luncheon drew to a close. Tracy provided Alice with lots of useful information on how to establish a support group for parents and friends of the LGBTQ community. As the students, alumni, and faculty left the room, Tracy and Alice continued to talk and to think of ways they could collaborate.

As Trevor's mom, Lila, was leaving the room, it occurred to Tracy to introduce Alice to Lila. The two women instantly recognized one another. They had grown up in neighboring towns only ten miles apart, and had known each other for many years. At the same time, Lila and Alice were beginning to realize that they hadn't actually known each other very well.

Lila proudly explained that the impetus for her personal transformation had been witnessing the love and respect between her son, Trevor, and his partner Chris. Lila's sincerity gave Alice the courage to disclose the many mistakes she felt she had made with her son who is gay. Alice described her naiveté, saying, "We had so little information when my son came out." She went on to say how deeply she regretted the way she had handled things, and that she feared her son could never forgive her. Her regret was the motivation for her desire to start an LGBTQ Support Group. "At least I can help other parents avoid the mistakes I made," she explained.

The room was nearly empty, and I was chatting with a few people when I noticed Tracy talking with Lila and Alice. I smiled as my eyes fell on Bria, Mark, and Jim who were still deep in conversation, and giggling as if they had known each other all their lives. As the three young people got up to leave, Jim turned around. He froze. Yet again! He stood there, frozen in his tracks, staring across the room. There, sitting with Tracy and Lila, was Jim's mother, Alice.

Alice looked up and saw Jim at the same instant that he noticed her. Their eyes locked and the years of pain shattered like glass. They reached for one another as tears spilled from their eyes. Mark put his arm around his new BFF Bria, and they stood shoulder to shoulder watching the pivotal moment between mother and son. It was so clearly a moment of acceptance. Jim and his mother had found each other, for the first time. We had just witnessed another powerful reunion.

7

CONCLUSION

THROUGH THE YEARS, I have given many lectures at various colleges. On one level, I am a person coming to the audience as the speaker. It makes me proud that many have shared comments how the information I have presented positively impacted their lives. On another level, those students attending have been the ones who have inspired me! I have watched, year after year, as timid freshman grew into confident, capable graduates. I have witnessed students who have transformed themselves from victims in their lives to powerful heroes and advocates for the rights of others.

In this book, I have shared my own coming-out story. I hope you can understand, from my experience, how important it is to connect with what is true about yourself. Your own coming-out experience may be very different from mine, but it is still so important that you respect and honor your own journey.

There were times when I felt very alone. I want you to know that this is a common experience for young people. Ironically, this feeling of isolation is one of the common threads that we share with each other. So, in the event that you are going through challenging times right now, please know that you are not alone. Be sure to reach out to others.

In Jim's story, you saw how people do not choose their sexual orientation. There are many factors that contribute to a person's sexual orientation, but conscious choice is simply not one of those factors. Knowing this will hopefully give you the confidence to embrace who you are. No matter who you are or what you stand for, you are worthy of unconditional love and acceptance.

In Bria's story, we learned about the mental health risks that many LGBTQ youth face when they are not able to be open and live their lives in an accepting environment. Through Bria's example, we saw how important it is to never give up hope. Hope is a powerful antidote to depression. Hope and love always trump hate and fear. So, no matter how bad things may seem, hang on, and reach out for help.

If you are in the middle of a challenging situation, I understand that it may be hard to believe that things will get better. But I have seen many people over the years who have moved through hopeless periods in life and gotten to a much better place. Often, our darkest hours provide us with the most powerful opportunities for deep growth. Never give up on yourself.

With Veronica, we explored the importance of assembling a team of supportive others around you. Life can be challenging if you are coming to terms with sexuality or gender identity issues, especially if what's true for you is not in sync with the predominant culture that surrounds you. You may not be able to change the opinions of your family members and friends, so be courageous and know that you can find and create a "family of choice" that includes people who will love and accept you as you are.

It's very important that you maintain a solid team of people who can help and support you. Your medical provider must be someone you can safely confide in. Your physical and mental health is of the greatest importance. You are a valuable person and the physical container that is your body deserves all the care and attention you would give your most prized possession.

If you are like Veronica and feel that you can't share information with your medical provider, please do whatever you can to find a provider with whom you can feel comfortable. Too many lives are lost because either people are afraid to share their stories with their medical providers or they are unable to find a more accepting medical provider. Don't let your story end because of that.

You cannot be all things to all people. No matter what, you can never please everyone all the time. In fact, it can be quite damaging to you if you sacrifice your integrity just so you can be liked by someone else.

If you are being bullied, it's really important to find supportive people who you can talk to about it. Perhaps you can connect with friends who are like-minded and tell them, or join a group at school that provides you with good support. You may need to find support for strengthening your self-worth from sources outside of the home. This might include neighbors, school counselors, teachers, or other important figures in your life.

Keep in mind, just at Chris did, that the person who is bullying you is putting their own struggles onto you. You are not under any type of legal contract that forces you to carry their junk for them. So let them have their own struggles. Let the bullying person go. You will be better off without them.

Whenever one person is put down or diminished, it truly does affect us all. Even when we're not conscious of each of those negative events, which are like the ripples in a pond, they do affect us. This is one reason I do what I do. Helping others to heal is also a way to continue healing myself.

When a young person grows and becomes able to embrace who they are, we all benefit. Not only people of the LGBTQ communities, but all people. I believe this is why many people who identify as "straight allies" of the LGBTQ communities devote themselves to furthering the rights of others. They know that we are all connected.

As the stories in this book have demonstrated, the deepest, most important periods of growth often germinate from the darkest, most intense challenges in life. Remember that you are never alone. People you have never met are pulling for you right now, including me.

Passing the Baton

I want to share one final story with you. Many years ago, my husband and I were struggling to find enough money to come up with a down payment for our first condo. We had pooled all our resources and tried everything we could think of, yet we were still coming up short.

I asked my parents for some financial help and, even though they had the resources, my father refused to help. Bill and I were therefore very close to losing our escrow on the condo when a colleague of mine stepped forward. She and I were in training together and she had only known me for a few months.

She called me one evening and offered to loan us the money we needed. She and her husband had never even met my husband, yet they were willing to help us out. Their act of generosity puzzled me, because I hadn't ever experienced generosity like that. I asked myself, *Why would someone I barely know be willing to help me like this?* Surely, there had to be strings attached.

The night the four of us met for us to receive the loan, my husband and I somewhat awkwardly asked, "Why? Why are you doing this for us?" Her reply has stuck with me ever since. She told us that no, there were no strings attached. The offer was just what it was; nothing more. It was an offer to help. She smiled warmly with compassion like I had never before experienced. Then she said something, which has become a guiding principle in my life. "Pay It Forward."

As you recall from Bria's story, the high school janitor, Dominga, and Bria's grandmother each passed on to Bria qualities that she would carry forward to advance the values of human dignity and growth for all people, regardless of gender identity or sexual orientation. Recall also Chris' mother, Maria, who had carried her parents' courage to stand up to an oppressive government. And then Chris passed the baton forward, helping others grow beyond what they had ever imagined they would be capable of.

Another motto for my work has been "compassion through education." I've been very fortunate to have had incredible mentors and teachers over the years. Many of those people were simply doing their jobs, doing what they had trained to do. Yet, each of them offered something more. They gave of themselves in ways that nourished my soul.

The work I do now is really an extension of those peoples' lives. They passed a baton to me and I am doing as much as I can to further human growth. So, now, as you read this, the baton is being passed on to you.

Now it is your journey that matters. You are being called to do your part. Your journey will be completely unique to you, and it is essential that you accept the mission that you have been given. Move forward with it. I invite you now to think about ways you can carry the baton and "pay it forward."

An important truth is that we can't heal if we're hiding. Another amazing truth I have learned is that a person heals the most when they work to help others heal. I'm excited for each of you as you begin your journey to healing.

* * *

It has been an honor and a privilege to write this book. Thank you for reading! I loved sharing my story with you and hope I'll have the opportunity to present in front of you one day.

REFERENCES

Chapter 2

[1] Bailey, J.; Pillard, R. (1991). A Genetic Study of Male Sexual Orientation. *Archives of General Psychiatry*. 48(12): 1089-1096.

[2] Blanchard, R. (2001). Fraternal Birth Order and the Maternal Immune Hypothesis of Male Homosexuality. *Hormones and Behavior*. 40 (2) 105-114.

[3] LeVay, S. (1991). A Difference in Hypothalamic Structure Between Homosexual and Heterosexual Men. *Science*. 253, 1034-1037.

[4] Savic, I.; Lindstrom, P. (2008). PET and MRI Show Differences in Cerebral Asymmetry and Functional Connectivity Between Homo- and Heterosexual Subjects. *Proceedings of National Academy of Sciences*. 105 (27) 9403-9408.

[5] Hamer, D. (1993). A Linkage Between DNA Markers on the X Chromosome and Male Sexual Orientation. *Science*. 261 (5119) 321-327.

* * *

Chapter 3

[6] Center for Substance Abuse Treatment (2009). Substance Abuse Treatment: Addressing the Specific Needs of Women. Rockville (MD): Substance Abuse and Mental Health Services Administration (US); (Treatment Improvement Protocol (TIP) Series, No. 51.) Chapter 6: Substance Abuse Among Specific Population Groups and Settings.

[7] Liu, R.; Mustanski, B. (2012). Suicidal Ideation and Self-Harm in Lesbian, Gay, Bisexual, and Transgender Youth. *American Journal of Preventive Medicine.* 42 (3) 221-228.

* * *

Chapter 4

[8] James, S. E., Herman, J. L., Rankin, S., Keisling, M., Mottet, L., & Ana , M. (2016). *The Report of the 2015 U.S. Transgender Survey.* Washington, DC: National Center for Transgender Equality.

[9] Murray, L. (2011, August 19). The High Price of Looking Like a Woman. *The New York Times.* Retrieved October 5, 2016, from www.nytimes.com.

[10] Allison, R. (2012, May). Ten Things Transgender Persons Should Discuss with Their Health Care Provider. *Gay and Lesbian Medical Association.* Retrieved October 22, 2016, from www.glma.org.

RESOURCES

Campus Pride – Organization whose primary objective is to develop necessary resources, programs and services to support LGBTQ and ally students on college campuses across the United States. www.campuspride.org

Gay & Lesbian Alliance Against Defamation (GLAAD) – Works with print, broadcast, and online news sources to bring people powerful stories from the LGBTQ community that build support for equality. GLAAD.org

Gay Lesbian Straight Education Network (GLSEN) – Strives to ensure that each member of every school community is valued and respected, regardless of sexual orientation or gender identity/expression. GLSEN.org

Gay Straight Alliance Network (GSA Network) – A GSA alliance is a student-run club, typically in a high school or middle school, that provides a safe place for students to meet, support each other, talk about issues related to sexual orientation and gender identity and expression, and work to end homophobia and transphobia. GSANetwork.org

Human Rights Campaign (HRC) – A national lesbian, gay, bisexual, transgender, and queer civil rights organization that envisions a world where LGBTQ people are ensured of their basic equal rights and can be open, honest, and safe at home, at work, and in the community. HRC.org

HRC Time to THRIVE Conference – The annual national conference to promote safety, inclusion, and well-being for LGBTQ youth everywhere. TimeToTHRIVE.org

It Gets Better Project – Their mission is to communicate to lesbian, gay, bisexual, and transgender youth around the world that it gets better, and to create and inspire the changes needed to make it better for them. ItGetsBetter.org

National Center for Lesbian Rights (NCLR) – A national legal organization committed to advancing the civil and human rights of lesbian, gay, bisexual, and transgender people and their families, through litigation, legislation, policy, and public education. NCLRights.org

PFLAG – Support for families, friends, and allies of people who are LGBTQ. PFLAG.org

The Trevor Project – Provides 24/7 crisis counseling to LGBTQ young people thinking of suicide; educates young people, and adults who interact with young people, on LGTBQ-competent suicide prevention, risk detection, and response. Call 1-866-488-7386 or go to TheTrevorProject.org.

Gay, Lesbian, Bisexual, and Transgender National Hotline (GLBT Hotline) – Provides vital peer support, community connections, and resource information to people with questions regarding sexual orientation and/or gender identity. Call 1-800-246-7743 or GLBTHotline.org.

ACKNOWLEDGMENTS

I'm grateful to my mom for the months of encouragement and emotional support she provided during the creation of this book. Fortunately she had the opportunity to read an advanced readers' copy before her passing. Her full support of this book's content means the world to me.

Thank you to my dearest and loving friend and mentor, Dr. Nancy Hebble, who helped me with editing this book in ways I never could. Her words of encouragement and support fueled me to move forward.

Much thanks to Joel and Heidi Roberts for video production and messaging.

I also wish to thank my friend and mentor, Marci Shimoff, who believed in me and my message before I did.

Thank you to Angela Lauria and her team for giving me the guidance and support to create a manuscript.

I am also grateful to Dr. Vincent Pompei for writing the foreword.

ABOUT THE AUTHORS

Dr. Ron Holt is a board-certified psychiatrist and a motivational speaker, author, and facilitator who resides in San Francisco, California. He is passionate about issues relevant to lesbian, gay, bisexual, transgender, and queer or questioning (LGBTQ) communities and is a leader in the LGBTQ happiness and mental health world.

Ron travels the country providing transformational education and mentoring to help people lead more authentic lives. He inspires people with breakthrough methods to help them achieve greater personal fulfillment. His style is approachable and relatable, and he is dedicated to helping people live more empowered and joy-filled lives.

Dr. William Huggett is a psychoanalyst and board-certified psychiatrist. He has a private practice where he focuses on helping individuals access the wealth of information and resources that exist within themselves. His goal is to help individuals be better equipped to live their lives aligned with their most authentic self. He helps clients develop their own tools including meditation, relaxation training, diet, physical exercise, and mindfulness techniques. You can find out more about Dr. Huggett by visiting his website: WilliamHuggett.com.

FOR MORE INFORMATION

I would love to speak at your school, University, or organization. You can contact me about speaking engagements, book signings, as well as view my videos, through my website at DrRonHolt.com.

In addition to an adult LGBTQ coloring book that complements this book, I am working on other writings and would like to send you the link for a free electronic version when released.

If you would like to receive a link for a free download of my coloring book, and/or receive updates on future writings or promotional events, please sign up at DrRonHolt.info.

You are worthy of unconditional love and acceptance – just the way you are. And remember to always be kind to one another.

23600537R00078

Made in the USA
San Bernardino, CA
03 February 2019